Myths
of the
Sacred
Tree

Myths *of the* Sacred Tree

Including Myths from *Africa, Native America, China, Sumeria, Russia, Greece, India, Scandinavia, Europe, Egypt, South America, Arabia*

MOYRA CALDECOTT

Illustrations by Anthea Toorchen

Destiny Books
Rochester, Vermont

Destiny Books
One Park Street
Rochester, Vermont 05767

Library of Congress Cataloging-in-Publication Data
Caldecott, Moyra
    Myths of the sacred tree / Moyra Caldecott.
      p. cm.
    Includes bibliographical references and index.
    ISBN 0-89281-414-4
    I. Trees—Mythology. I. Title.
  BL325. P7C35 1993
  291.2'12—dc20   93-11201
                                                  CIP

Printed and bound in the United States

10 9 8 7 6 5 4 3 2 1

Text design by Randi Jinkins

Destiny Books is a division of Inner Traditions International

Distributed to the book trade in the United States by American Interna-tional Distribution Corporation (AIDC)

Distributed to the book trade in Canada by Publishers Group West (PGW), Montreal West, Quebec

Distributed to the book trade in the United Kingdom by Deep Books, London

Distributed to the book trade in Australia by Millennium Books, Newtown, N. S. W.

Permission to reproduce e. e. cumming's poem granted by Liveright Pub-lishing Company, New York

For Benjamin, Tessa, Sophie, and Rosie
With hope that they will grow up in a world with trees

Tree

The spread of this tree
out-domes St. Paul's . . .
Entering is initiation.
Leaving,
transformation.

The power of this tree
out-drives
man's ambition to the moon . . .
pumps life through every cell
and outlives history.

Without enmity
its strength
can crack mountains . . .
tumble cities . . .
yet here it holds so still
and silent
that the frailest butterfly
is not afraid
to ride its shining leaves.

M.C.

Florence

God is not here
in these dim churches.
He waits in the chestnut tree
to catch the tourist unawares . . .
springing on him
in the flicker of light
between leaves.
Those dead artists —
the best of them —
knew it
and always placed a tree
somewhere behind the solemn group
of protagonists
as a sly nod to the true pilgrim . . .

M.C.

i thank You God for most this amazing
day: for the leaping greenly spirits of trees
and a blue true dream of sky; and for everything
which is natural which is infinite which is yes

e. e. cummings, from Xaipe

Contents

Introduction

The natural world, specifically the tropical rain forest, has been described in a way that harmonizes very well with the view of the spiritual world expressed symbolically in so many ancient myths and legends. It is "a living miracle of complexity," and the canopy of the rain forest is "translucent, the light declining steadily in intensity as it filters through the leaves. This mass of vegetation offers opportunities for life to plants adapted to different and very specific degrees of illumination. . . . Different tree species slot their adult crowns into the canopy at different heights depending on their physiological needs. Clinging to their branches and leaves, or to each other, are lesser plants which share their preferences—lichen and mosses, ferns and orchids in great and varied profusion. Interwoven within and draped across the canopy are the stems and foliage of climbing palms and lianas, which help to bind the forest into a continuous physical structure. . . . In this intimidatingly diverse and dynamic environment, most of the action is hidden from view. . . ." (Julian Caldecott, in *The Rainforests*, Lisa Silcock, ed.).

I hope my scientist son will forgive me quoting him out of context to illustrate a point. I don't think he would object to the anal-

ogy between the forest and life in general which latter is certainly "a miracle of complexity" in which the intensity of mental and spiritual illumination declines the further one gets from the source. As one travels further from the unimaginable origin of ultimate light above the crown of the mystic tree, vision is dimmer, the way harder, the life-forms more adapted purely to physical and material reality—some so well adapted to the dark regions that they hardly miss the light at all. The rich and diverse nature of the forest, in which everything is dependent on everything else, though of different forms and subject to different needs, gives us a pool of images and symbols for the greater and multidimensional life we can now only see "through a glass darkly" but which we believe to exist. There are symbols and metaphors in this fertile natural phenomenon to serve all levels of experience, from the grossest to the most rarified.

Most of the important action in our lives is hidden from view, taking place on the spiritual plane, for what we do there affects events far beyond the areas our limited physical minds can grasp. We have to preserve our physical world, the environment our bodies need to survive on this earth, but we also must preserve the secret and invisible world, the environment our spirits need to survive in eternity. The tree is essential to one, and the symbol of the tree is essential to the other. The physical tree sustains our bodies with its fruit, its shade, its capacity to reproduce oxygen and to hold the fertile soil safe. The mythic tree sustains our spirit with its constant reminder that we need both the earth and the sunlight—the physical and the spiritual—for full and potent life. The tree gives us a sense of quiet continuity, for its life is long compared with ours, and it is not inconceivable that we might sit in the shade of the same tree to contemplate the meaning of life that Shakespeare himself sat under to compose *Hamlet*. Some trees live thousands of years; archaeologists today use the growth rings in ancient bristle-cone pines from California and ancient oaks preserved in Irish bogs to date the major events of the past, much as radiocarbon dating techniques have been used. It is possible from tree-ring evidence to know almost exactly when a major catastrophe, such as a huge volcanic eruption, happened half a world away. The alteration in world climate is registered in the tree's growth for the year.

The tree re-creates itself continually. It dies. Its body fertilizes the earth from which its seed springs into new life. Nothing is wasted. Everything is recycled. Are we, too, not part of life's rich cyclic pattern? It is inconceivable that after a lifetime of careful and painful progress toward an understanding of ourselves and our universe that the very consciousness so long in evolving should be snuffed out and wasted senselessly like nothing else in nature. Surely our spirit, the seed that contains all our potential, will grow again.

"Just as the seed contains the tree, and the tree the seed, so the hidden world of God contains all Creation, and Creation is, in turn, a revelation of the hidden world of God" (Roger Cook, *The Tree of Life*, p. 18).

When we talk about the spirit, our ordinary language is inadequate, because we don't know exactly what the spirit is, though—to use again the analogy of the forest—when we see leaves moving on a tree we assume the possible existence of a breeze, and even so do we assume the existence of spirit because of certain otherwise inexplicable experiences in our lives. The language we use when we attempt to talk about spirit is of necessity highly symbolic.

The symbol of the tree, almost more than any other, lifts us from the familiar to the divine.

One of the most magnificent symbolic structures the floundering mind of man has ever conceived to explain the inexplicable is the mystical sefirotic tree of life of the kabbalists, the Jewish mystics. Halevi's *A Kabbalistic Universe* gives us a brief glimpse of the mighty tree of life:

> God is God and there is nothing to compare with God . . . therefore no attributes can be given to this Absolute.
>
> God willed to see God and so God's Will, symbolized by light, shone. . . .
>
> God willed the first separation so that God might behold God. This . . . was accomplished by a contraction in Absolute All, so as to make a place wherein the mirror of Existence might manifest.
>
> The first Light, or first Sefirah, as this manifestation of Divinity is called, is the seed of all that was, is and shall be. It is the Light from which all other Lights, or Sefirot, emanate.
>
> When God willed the world to come into being, the seed took root and grew downward into the trunk, branch and fruit of a

Divine Tree that would act as an intermediary between the World
and God. . . . (pp. 7-9).

The tree of life grows through four "worlds," or realms. The
topmost is closest to the Divine: the thought before the word, as
it were. The ten major Hebrew names of God may be sought here,
the Trinity of the Christians, likewise. In the second region, we find
the mighty archangels and archetypes; in the third, the angels and
elementals. The fourth is our world of material reality and physical being. The lowest region of this, even further from the source,
is the chasm where dark forces unmotivated by the desire to rejoin the source of light exist.

Through these four realms the great tree stretches out its
branches with the ten sefirot, or shining spheres, or vortexes of
divine energy. It is through these four realms that we make our
great and difficult journey of the spirit.

The schematic tree of the kabbalists contains ten points of divine emanation, or sefirah, to which and from which the original
impulse of light from God passes, and an eleventh that is too mysterious even for symbolic representation—the inconceivable Holy
Spirit. These sefirot represent "the Divine attributes, powers and
potencies" (Cook, p. 19), arranged in groups of three: thesis, antith-
esis, synthesis; male, female, neuter; active, passive, potential.

"The World is sustained by the Will and Grace of God. Until
God ends Time the emanated Tree of the Sefirot will exist for
ever" (Halevi, p. 19).

This divine tree is at once mystically rooted in heaven, growing downward toward our world, and rooted in the world growing upward toward heaven. There is a flow from above to below
and from below to above: a continual spiral movement of energy
from God and toward God. The movement alternates as it rises
and falls and rises again from one side of the tree to the other, one
side representing the active drive of will, the other the restrictive
or passive energy that holds the whole in balance. Without the
trunk of equilibrium, the branches cannot exist. Without the
branches, the diversity of God's creation—ranging from the darkest souls in the regions furthest from the light to such mighty shining beings as the archangels closest to the source of light—cannot
move freely about the tree. Without the branches, the tree is limited and limiting.

The kabbalists were not the only religious philosophers to use the symbol of the tree inverted to express divinity's descent into materiality and materiality's subsequent climb to divinity. In the Hindu religion the *Katha Upanishad* (ca. 900–500 B.C.E.) states: "This eternal asvattha whose roots rise on high and whose branches grow low is the pure, the Brahman, what is called non-Death. All the worlds rest in it." Again, in the *Maitreya Upanishad,* we are told "the Threefold Brahman has its roots above" and in the branching of this tree we see that though there are many gods, they are but branches of "a single, hidden root" (Cook, p. 18).

Mircea Eliade, authoritative writer and lecturer on the history of religions, points out in his excellent book *Shamanism* (p. 272) that the symbolism of the cosmic tree is almost inexhaustible. In writing about Asiatic tribes in Siberia and Oceania he describes a tree symbolism not far from the kabbalist's vision. Behind all "the gods" there is almost always a Supreme God: "He Who has His beginning in Himself" (p. 286).

The tree is essential to the work of the tribal shaman. "From its wood he makes his drum" which induces trance and thus helps him to contact the spiritual worlds. On the surface of the drum he often depicts an inverted tree. In his initiation and later rituals he climbs the birch tree, "the guardian of the door to the sky." He effectually reaches the summit of the cosmic tree, which rises at the center of the world, the place of the earth's "umbilicus," and connects the three cosmic regions, its branches touching the sky and its roots going down into the underworld.

"Several religious ideas are implied in the symbolism of the World Tree," says Eliade. "On the one hand it presents the universe in continual regeneration, the inexhaustible spring of cosmic life, the paramount reservoir of the sacred . . . on the other, it symbolizes our contact with the sky. . . . Enriched by innumerable mythical doublets and complementary symbols . . . the Cosmic Tree always presents itself as the very reservoir of life and the master of destinies" (Eliade, p. 271).

"The Yakut believe that at the 'golden navel of the earth' stands a tree with eight branches; it rises in a sort of primordial paradise, for there the first man was born and he feeds on the milk of a woman who half emerges from the trunk of the tree" (Eliade, p. 272). When I first read this, my mind jumped at once to ancient Egypt, where Hathor, the goddess of love and fertility, feeds the pharaoh with milk from her breasts emerging from the trunk of a sycamore fig tree. Myth is never bounded by time or space. Wherever and whenever we need a symbol for a spiritual matter we draw on the same nature that surrounds us, whether in Siberia, Egypt, or South America.

"Nothing that is said is any more than a symbol for a reality that the natural mind cannot ever comprehend. If however there is a shift, a lift in the perception of the reader, then the image may dissolve to reveal that reality" (Halevi, p. 4).

If we move away from the divine tree of life that suggests so vividly the dynamic relationship between God and creation—the link between divinity and materiality, the subtle and constant movement between above and below, and below and above—we find the symbolism of trees used in many different ways throughout the world.

The ancient Celts had a particular approach, more personal and magical rather than metaphysical and mystical. The stone circles often associated with the druid priesthood were in fact ancient before ever the Celts and their druid priests came to Britain. The sacred sites of the druids were always groves and woods, and just about every indigenous tree had a magical significance for them.

Robert Graves, in his extraordinary and confusing book *The White Goddess,* writes confidently about an ancient Celtic tree alphabet. Many writers since have used his version as an authoritative text on Celtic tree lore, while others have scorned it and produced their own versions. To the ancient Celts, each tree represented a period of time in the wheel of the year—hence we speak of the Celtic tree calendar. But each tree also represented aspects of the nature of humanity and of gods so clearly and specifically that a system of divination was devised that rings true even today.

An ancient Egyptian concept, depicted on many temple walls, was that the god Djehuti (Thoth) writes the name of the pharaoh on the leaves of the cosmic persea tree to insure his immortality. "Among the Osmanti Turks," writes Mircea Eliade, "the Tree of Life has a million leaves, on each of which a human fate is written: each time a man dies, a leaf falls. The Ostyak believe that a goddess seated on a seven-storey celestial mountain, writes a man's fate, as soon as he is born, on a tree with seven branches . . . "

6

(Eliade, p. 273). When the shaman, using all his powers of magic and esoteric knowledge, finally reaches the summit of the cosmic tree, having journeyed through all the different realms and finally reaching the last heaven, he asks for knowledge of the future and the fate of the soul. Why do we call a diagram of our family history a tree?

The tree is at once a ladder on which the soul climbs to the celestial regions and a book on the leaves of which is written the wisdom of the ages and the final truth we all have to face. No longer can we hide behind distortions of the truth, half-truths, and falsehoods. The living leaves of the cosmic tree, growing as they do from the source of light, give us reality *as it is* without interference from irresponsible and ill-intentioned writers, editors, teachers, preachers, and television presenters!

Frightened by the immensity of the universe and the mystery of our being here at all, we have always needed to understand the meaning of our lives. The most effective approach to this impossible task since cave-dwelling times has been the medium of story—deeply significant, symbolic story. The ancient myths and legends have been effective through hundreds, sometimes thousands, of generations, but recently they have been set aside in favor of scientific and technological knowledge. This approach has ultimately proved to be unsatisfactory, and more and more people are looking for a deeper meaning to their lives that will be untouched by nuclear and other man-made disasters. The ancient stories are being recognized now for what they always were: symbolic guides to an inner journey toward understanding and transforming the self through the dawning of spiritual awareness.

The Dyak of Malaysia believe that the first pair of ancestors was born from the tree of life (Eliade, p. 273), and in Africa we can find the same myth. There is a pygmy story that goes something like this:

A chameleon standing on a branch one day, swaying forward and swaying back, watching a fly settle on a leaf, heard a strange twittering or whispering, a strange rippling and gurgling.

"What is that?" he asked himself.

At this time on earth there was no water to make this sound of water, and the chameleon did not know what to think.

The fly that was to have made a tasty meal for the chameleon flew away, and the chameleon had nothing now to distract him from his curiosity.

At last he fetched an axe and split the tree open.

Out of the gash flooded water. It gushed and rushed and flowed, soon filling the valleys and after the valleys the great low places to become lakes and seas. Two strange beings were washed out of the tree with the water. Two such beings the chameleon had never seen. He stared and stared. And they in turn stared back, for they had never seen such a world.

They were the first man and woman, and they were born from a tree. (Geoffrey Parrinder, *African Mythology,* p. 45.)

The Herero tribe of southwest Africa have a similar myth. They believed that at the time of the beginning, the first man and woman came out of the omumborumbonga tree. This tree is now sacred. The people bow to it reverently and scatter offerings of herbs and grass over its roots. They even speak to it as to their mother and their father, praying for whatever they need. It is taboo to sit in the shade of it and gossip, for it is a holy tree and its shadow creates a holy place.

We may not today believe that the first man and woman were born from a tree, but remembering what we have already said about the tree representing the union of earth and heaven, and the two-way flow of energy between the spiritual and the material world, we can respond easily to the esoteric meaning of the story.

We would do well to remember that trees were on earth long before we were. We should respect them, and it would do us no harm to believe that the shade around a tree is a sacred space, a space where we can rest and be quiet and contemplate with amazement and gratitude the fact of our being alive on this earth at all. I am sure we have all had experiences of a profound nature sitting under a tree, from a sudden and overwhelming conviction that God really does exist to a less transcendental but nevertheless important conviction that *we* exist in a way we had never dreamed of before.

Oft have I stood
Foot-bound, uplooking at this lovely Tree
Beneath a frosty moon. The hemisphere

8

~ Introduction ~

Of magic fiction, verse of mine perhaps
May never tread; but scarcely Spenser's self
Could have more tranquil visions in this youth,
More bright appearances could scarcely see
Of human Forms with superhuman powers,
Than I beheld, standing on winter nights
Alone, beneath this fairy work of earth.
    —*from William Wordsworth,* The Prelude

There should be some such word as stat-esthetic awareness, as well as kin-esthetic, for in addition to a sense of movement, the body has an architectural sense of forces in equilibrium, thrust and counterthrust—the delicate adjustments required for keeping perfectly still. Sitting here in the dark at the foot of this tree . . . I notice that in my own statesthetic and kinesthetic awareness of the body I continue to feel, in defiance of my education, that the center of the universe is right here, in my own center of gravity, and that I am surrounded by a sphere whose radius is the limit of my vision in every direction.
    —from Martha Heyneman, "Dante's Magical Memory Cathedral"

There is no doubt that in ancient pagan times, as well as more recently in so-called primitive societies, when trees and forests were considered divine and inhabited by spirits and various orders of sacred beings, nature stood a much better chance of survival in its original and beautiful state. The early church directed a lot of its energy to cutting down sacred groves and trees in order to drive people into the church, and science has added its bit by analyzing the tree—root, branch, and cell—and finding in the material components no sign of a spirit or an elemental. When scientists have succeeded in finding out exactly what life is—what *exactly* is the difference between animate and inanimate, alive and dead—I'll feel more confident in their pronouncements on this matter. What we still don't know still outweighs what we do know, and the mystic symbol, the myth-making faculty, is still the only means we have so far of squaring our inexplicable, but nevertheless real, experiences with the unknown.

Even today, after all these years of brainwashing by the rationalists, materialists, and scientists, we still feel good when we put our arms around a tree. We still feel our troubled thoughts fall into place and a great surge of confidence in the reality of something

9

beyond our ken. I have seen pebbles and pieces of rag hung on trees, each representing a secret prayer for help or a private thank-you for help received. The forest heals, not only with the numerous compounds the drug companies find growing there, and not only by supplying us with oxygen and by holding the rich topsoil of our planet in place, but because it heals our spirit. Even the Christians who cut down the sacred groves must have felt the loss, because they built their cathedrals with soaring columns like the trunks of trees and with vaulted ceilings ribbed and fanned like the canopy of a forest, and everywhere, in unexpected places, they carved the head of the Green Man—the spirit of nature—peering out of his leafy dell, beautiful and challenging.

William Anderson, in his excellent book *Green Man: The Archetype of Our Oneness with the Earth,* writes: "An archetype can be thought of according to the older use of the term as one of the eternal ideas of Platonic and Neo-Platonic philosophy and therefore as an ever living, vital and conscious force, or in the sense in which Jung made use of it as an image from the collective unconscious of humanity. According to both these theories an archetype such as the Green Man represents will recur at different places and times independently of traceable lines of transmission because it is part of the permanent possession of mankind. In Jung's theory of compensation, an archetype will reappear in a new form to redress imbalances in society at a particular time when it is needed. According to this theory, therefore, the Green Man is rising up into our present awareness in order to counterbalance a lack in our attitude to Nature" (chap. 1). "An archetype when expressed through great art not only reveals many layers of meanings: it also faces us with far more mysteries than we ever would have suspected" (chap. 6).

Carl Jung said, in *Man and His Symbols,* that "an ancient tree . . . represents symbolically the growth and development of the psychic life (as distinct from instinctual life, commonly symbolized by animals)" (p. 153). "The further we delve into the origins of a 'collective image' . . . the more we uncover a seemingly unending web of archetypal patterns that, before modern times, were never the object of conscious reflection. . . . In former times men did not reflect upon their symbols; they lived them and were unconsciously animated by their meaning" (p. 81).

Even today, everything we do, everything we think, everything we are is influenced subliminally by the background mythical traditions of our culture and, beyond that, by the universal mythical traditions of the human race.

We stand in a garden at dawn and are moved by a feeling we cannot put into words. if we care to analyze the feeling (though it were better we did not), we find we are influenced by a great many things besides the actual physical nature of what we experience. "In the beginning . . . " we hear somewhere deep inside us as we react to the beginning of a new day, and the story of the miracle of the creation is ours to draw upon: the only true miracle, the bringing out of nothing of all that is. We take a deep breath and remember subliminally the breath of God giving Adam life. We are cleansed by it, reborn, renewed. And then a tree rustles in the breeze and again subliminally we remember the tree of life, the tree of knowledge, and the freedom we have to obey or disobey. Some small creature rustles in the grass and we shiver, remembering the serpent in Eden, temptation, the pain and suffering that go inseparably with the knowledge of good and evil. A bird wings past; it is black and we remember the raven; another, and we hear in the beating of its wings the messenger dove with the green leaf in its beak returning to the ark, the dove of the Holy Spirit descending upon the Christ, the promise. Someone calls our name from the house and we are expected to join other people, have breakfast, cope with rush hour, work, city life. Our name is called and we are expected. We will need the strength that we have received from the secret messages of the myth.

We read a story and an article. The article lies on the page and scarcely moves, but the story drops like a pebble into a pool and causes ripples to spread out in ever-widening circles from the center, the effect of it far beyond what is on the page, growing all the time in our mind. The writer of the story has used word and phrase to hint, to suggest, to lead our mind back to an ancient archetype or legend that will help us, at our own pace and in our own way, reach whatever point we need to reach at that time. The writer has written a multileveled story, which unfolds and unfolds in our mind long after the first reading. The same kind of secret code is being used as that which worked for us in the garden at dawn, though neither the writer nor we, the reader, may consciously realize it. The myth has had a subliminal effect. How much primal fear arises in us when the writer uses the word "dark," for instance? How much of comfort in divine harmony unfolds with the word "light" or "spiral" or "circle" or "whole"?

A myth clothes those deep and mysterious insights into the meaning of life that we all have but sometimes refuse to recognize. Mythic truth is the language of the inner journey, and it cannot be judged by the same criteria we use in a court of law or in a laboratory. It has to sound true against our hearts. It has to fall into place like a rolling ball into the hole that was designed for it.

"Many a truth is to be found hidden beneath a covering of fiction," said Theodolphus, Bishop of Orleans at the time of Charlemagne.

A few years ago I woke one morning with the sensation that words were being spoken through me and I ought to write them down. I was very sleepy and didn't want to wake, so I turned over and went back to sleep. The words came again and again until at last, groaning, I reached for pen and paper and wrote them down. At the time I was not aware of what I was writing, but on reading the words when fully awake I found that I had written this:

> Atman was given the secret of the universe as a gift. He was pleased, but he didn't know what to do with it. At first he tested it in all kinds of ways to find out what it was, but failing to get a satisfactory answer he played with it as though it were a bauble or a toy. Eventually he hung it on a tree as decoration. And then he forgot it.
>
> So it stayed for a long time . . . an unconsidered trifle . . . until one day someone came by who recognised it and asked if he might have it.
>
> Atman gladly parted with it in exchange for an artifact and went off satisfied that he had struck a good bargain, rejoicing in his newly acquired treasure.
>
> The one who now had the secret of the universe saw that it was a seed and planted it in his garden. It grew to be the Tree of Life and he sat in its shade in the heat of the day and was filled with great reverence and love.
>
> All things were clear to him.
> All things were good.
>
> Meanwhile Atman began to grow dissatisfied and miserable. The artifact no longer pleased him. He was bored with it. He had

done whatever there was to be done with it on the first day and thereafter he could find out nothing new about it.

The man who had the Secret of the Universe however was never bored, its variations were infinite, his interest in it ever deepening.

At last Atman, having realised his mistake came to the man and asked for it back. But now the price was so high Atman could not pay it.

He went away and worked for endless aeons to earn the price of the thing he had sold so carelessly and so cheaply before. "When I get it back," he thought, "I will never let it go, for indeed, it is the only thing worth having."

At that moment the man standing under the Tree of Life reached out to him and gave him freely of its fruit.
—from Moyra Caldecott, *Child of the Dark Star*

According to M.-L. von Franz, "our dream life creates a meandering pattern in which individual strands or tendencies become visible, then vanish, then return again. If one watches this meandering design over a long period of time, one can observe a sort of hidden regulating or directing tendency at work, creating a slow, imperceptible process of psychic growth—the process of individuation" (M.-L. von Franz, "The Process of Individuation," in Carl G. Jung, *Man and His Symbols*, p. 161).

Jung called the organizing center the "self" and described it as the totality of the whole psyche, in order to distinguish it from the "ego," which constitutes only a small part of the total psyche. "The Greeks called it man's inner *daimon*, in Egypt it was expressed by the concept of the *Ba-soul*; and the Romans worshipped it as the "genius" native to each individual. In more primitive societies it was often thought of as a protective spirit embodied within an animal or a fetish" (M.-L. von Franz, p. 161).

Some people today, including myself, tend to use the words "higher self" or "higher consciousness" and "lower" or "little" self or "lower" or "ordinary" consciousness.

"Since . . . psychic growth cannot be brought about by a conscious effort of will power, but happens involuntarily and naturally, it is in dreams frequently symbolized by the tree, whose slow, powerful, involuntary growth fulfills a definite pattern" (M.-L. von Franz, p. 161).

Innumerable myths and legends trace the progress of this individuation process—this finding of the higher self, this recognition of that part of oneself that climbs the tree of life seeking union with its original source.

At the very top one visualizes the fully realized higher self, like a bird looking back, and sees for the first time the whole pattern laid out beneath it so that at last everything makes sense. Then, in a blaze of light, it becomes subsumed or dissolved into the one from which it has been so long exiled.

But meanwhile, during the process of individuation or progress toward finding one's higher self, the lower self can play a damaging role in setting up obstacles. The lower self wants comfort, familiarity, security. It does not want adventures of a spiritual nature. It does not want danger or challenging situations. It does not want to have anything to do with something it does not immediately understand. Only when this lower self is prepared, at the very least, to stop frustrating the higher self in its efforts can real progress be made.

If we needed further proof that trees have inspired us for centuries with feelings of the sacred, the numinous, and the spiritually potent, we need look no further than the literature and art connected with mazes. These extraordinary patterns are no more the playgrounds of children than are myths themselves.

As we walk a maze and stop short time and again with the realization that we have taken a wrong turn and are further from our destination than before, we recognize that we have entered an ancient archetype and are acting out the drama of ourselves lost in a bewildering universe, where our physical limitations keep us from seeing further than our own noses.

In Vao, in the New Hebrides, even today it is believed that the spirit of a man arrives before the entrance to a sea-cave where the fearful "guardian ghost" has traced an elaborate pattern in the sand, a path for him to follow. At his approach she obliterates half of the design, which the dead man must complete or be devoured. If he has danced with the tribe as an initiate of the higher mysteries and has now remembered the steps, he has no problem. If he has not, he is lost. The dance we dance during our life is the one that will make the difference in our future at death. Life is learned in the steps of a dance whose pattern is half drawn on the sands of time, half in our eternal souls (based on Rachel Levy, *The Gate of Horn*).

ᴥ Introduction ᴥ

Mazes have symbolized the spiritual path since time immemorial.

There are basically two major types of maze or labyrinth. One is designed to cause us agitation and anxiety by showing us how easy it is to get lost. Our worst nightmares of meeting a devouring monster (a minotaur?) while we are lost come to haunt us. But another type is designed to have the opposite effect, and at its center there is very often a tree—a tree whose branches rustle in the wind for everyone to see and hear, but which has as much undergound—silent, invisible, powerfully sustaining and nourishing—as it has above. This type of maze has a single path, which winds to the center. The purpose of it is to slow us down, not to lose us. We cannot stride purposefully straight toward our goal; we have to walk around and around, back and forth. By the time we reach the center the irritating chatter of our minds is stilled and the worries of the world are forgotten. When we reach the center we should be ready for deep and leisurely meditation. For this reason many churches and cathedrals adopted this ancient figuration and marked it on the flagstones at the entrance to their holy space. Chartres Cathedral, in France, and Ely Cathedral, in Cambridgeshire, England, are well-known examples of this.

D. M. Dooling writes, "If any clue is given that can lead us out of the labyrinth of appearances, it is in the myths and fairy tales that should reach us—if parents are wise and children lucky—at almost the same time that the appearances become familiar, so that how things look is united in the developing consciousness with the real meaning of their hidden dimensions. Otherwise, there awaits the painful process of either bringing the opposites together as we grow older, or of living our lives with a one-sided—or more exactly, a one-dimensional—version of reality. For it is not that appearances are in themselves false; they are indeed a part, but only a part, of what things are. The falsity consists in the impression that they are the total truth" (Dooling, "The Mythic Dimension," *Parabola* IX, no. 4 [1984]: 41).

Anne Twitty says, "I turned back to myth, apocrypha, fairy tales, finding in them a truth that ran like a silver thread through and past the condescension that surrounded them" (Twitty, "Seven Long Years Riding Through the Dark Wood," *Parabola* XI, no. 4 [1986]: 12). Fairy stories heard as a child are "forgotten," yet their magic still works for us subliminally. They are part of our lives—affecting them and changing them. The tree image we take into

15

ourselves and it grows there giving us new and potent visions on which to feed.

In several of my own novels, notably *The Green Lady and the King of Shadows* and *The Tower and the Emerald*, I draw deeply on myth. In the latter I use the legend that an emerald fell from the crown of Lucifer when he was expelled from heaven. In the story it is a kind of grail, the human protagonists believing that they can restore the balance of the two major forces—dark and light, good and evil, creation and destruction—if they can only find the emerald.

A sound made them return their attention to earth. Standing at the edge of the lake, with the silver water lapping about her feet, stood the Green Lady, tall as a young rowan tree, her robe of leaves rustling around her, cornflowers and the magical five-pointed periwinkle in her hair. She was reaching out her hand to them in greeting, and as her sleeve fell aside, they could see the fine silver-green of her arm. Then she began to sing, her voice hauntingly sad.

She sang of a love she had once had long ago . . . of how they had lived in peace and harmony . . . of how each and every being had enjoyed a place to be and purpose to pursue . . . how each and every being had flourished in harmony with each and every other. . . . Then—and her tune grew more measured, more sombre—her lover had cut down the forests and drained the lakes; had ripped open the hills and covered the fields so that no living thing could grow there. . . . He had wanted control. He had wanted power. Eventually he had power over all things . . . but it gave him no joy. . . . For what he had power over had been changed out of all recognition. . . .

Angrily he had left her. . . .

Now she was going to call him back. . . .

The notes of her song flew out over the lake like silver birds. The hills gave back an echo as fine as harp music. They could hear the yearning in her heart. They could hear the name she called. . . .

Ny-ak appeared, tall and gaunt, his eyes hollow, his limbs like the charred branches of a tree that has been struck by lightning.

"Why do you call, woman?" he asked coldly. "We have nothing to say to each other." His voice rumbled across the lake like thunder, and they could see dark clouds gathering on the horizon. A wind sprang up and the reeds at the water's edge were shaken like spears before a battle.

"If only we still had the emerald," whispered Viviane, moving close to Caradawc. They could feel it—the coming conflict.

So the two great angels confronted each other. How could he resist her, Viviane thought: she was as beautiful as a summer's day in a green and temperate land. But he was angry. His human vehicle had deserted him; he had been crossed and thwarted at every turn. He was in no mood for overtures of peace. He raised his finger and pointed at the sun. A black cloud covered it instantly, and from that cloud poured down a thousand demons of darkness—tearing, biting, snapping, screaming, shrieking . . . while the four humans clung desperately to the oak tree at the water's edge to prevent themselves being swept away.

But the Green Lady turned her shoulder to the onslaught and summoned up her own forces. The sun was cleared of cloud again, and from the horizon of the dawn came a host of beings as clear as crystal, as refreshing as rain, spreading a net over the earth which, where it was touched, sprang into leafy growth—and the demons caught in it were turned to stone. . . .

Ny-ak watched the blessed transformation with bitter anger.

He raised his arms on high and a whirlwind of foul air lifted up the grains of sand, the rocks, the twigs, the leaves, hurling them higher and higher until a solid tower of darkness stood beside them on the shore.

Caradawc held Viviane close.

There were no windows in the tower. Only a door.

The Green Lady stooped and cast a small object at the tower's base. They could not discern it, but it must have been a seed—for the foundations began to crack and a green shoot began pushing through the rock. Fissures spread rapidly, and from every one a growing leaf-bud emerged, until the tower had become a living tree. . . .

Ny-ak scowled darkly and drew the sword from the scabbard at his side. No lightning flash was ever as livid as the light that burned from the blade. The tree was felled . . . the tower with it . . . the earth shuddering to receive the debris.

She lifted the lake in her long hands as though it were a cloak of silver silk. She threw it upwards—and as it floated in the air, it rained down a myriad fishes of diamond and amethyst. Then it fell on the flashing sword and clung to it, entangling Ny-ak's arm and impeding his movements.

Cursing, he shook himself free, the sword clattering to the ground wrapped in the embracing silk.

"Ny-ak," she cried. "Why do you fight me? We could be lovers and all the world would benefit. . . . "

"Woman . . . I need power. How could I accept an equal?"

"Then you will never know love at all," she answered sadly.

She turned away from him and took a step on to the dry bed of the lake.

Watching, Viviane and the others saw her pause and then, before their eyes, take root and turn into a tree.

Astonished, they looked back at Ny-ak. Where he had been, another blind tower had risen on the ruins of the old.

—from *The Tower and the Emerald*

The diversity of our use of the tree as meaningful metaphor and symbol knows no end.

The book you are reading is not a story book—it is *about* stories. I have given only the bare bones of the traditional myths and legends. The value of the book is that it gathers together some of the ancient myths and legends about trees and draws attention to their connection with our deepest spiritual needs. To cut down a forest is to harm ourselves as much as it denudes the earth of a much-needed resource and a marvelous beauty.

A lifetime of reading is behind this book. The Selected Bibliography at the end lists the books I have most recently consulted on the subject. At the end of each story, I acknowledged my immediate source for that particular story.

My gratitude goes to all who have contributed to my instruction over the years, and my apologies to those who have not been specifically named.

Gilgamesh and the Cedar Forest

Sumerian

Enlil, the right hand of Anu the limitless one; Enlil the mover on the face of the ocean; Enlil the breath of the earth—Enlil took Gilgamesh aside and spoke his destiny.

"You shall be a mighty king, a chosen one, a man who will do great deeds that other men will try to emulate. Take care that you use the power I give you well."

And Gilgamesh became king of Uruk, and Gilgamesh did great deeds.

But Gilgamesh the king was restless, and the great goddess made him a friend and companion as energetic as himself. His name was Enkidu.

One day Gilgamesh said to his friend Enkidu, "I have not done enough. I desire to make my name ring among the generations not yet born. I desire to set my name up where no man has set his name before. I will go to the land of the living, to the cedar forests, and I will build a monument that will last forever."

Enkidu warned him that Enlil had appointed a fearsome giant, Humbaba, armed with sevenfold terrors, to guard the forests. "His voice can be heard above the roar of the storm, yet he contains a silence in which the smallest movement of a deer sixty leagues distant can be heard."

"You can walk behind me if you are afraid," said Gilgamesh. "But I will meet this watchman of the forest. My name will go down through the generations as the one who defeated the undefeated—as the one who created a monument to outlast all others."

Enkidu could not dissuade his companion from the enterprise, but he persuaded him at least to seek the help of Shamash, the sun god. The king listened to this advice and went before the sun god to tell him of his intentions and to ask his protection.

"Why, Gilgamesh? Why do you want to do this?" Shamash asked.

Gilgamesh replied, "In the city the lives of men are circumscribed. Our names are lost in the crowd. Our breaths are achieved with struggle. We die in despair having achieved nothing."

Shamash was still not convinced.

"If it is not my destiny to go to the land of the cedar and do this deed," Gilgamesh cried, "why have you put this restlessness in my heart? Why have you stirred my dreams and awakened my yearning?"

So Shamash accepted the pleas of Gilgamesh and promised him help, giving him the eight great winds to be his warriors. The king went to the forge and gave orders that his weapons and his armor should be made under his direction, mightier than any that had ever been made before.

Gilgamesh spoke to his people and told them he was going to show the world the strength of the king of Uruk and leave behind him a name that would never be forgotten. His counsellors warned him that no man could find his way in the forest, which was ten thousand leagues in every direction. They warned him that no man could defeat Humbaba.

But Gilgamesh laughed.

"What shall I do then—sit at home in safety all my days? Come, Enkidu," he said, "we will go to Ninsun, my mother, and ask her for directions so that we will not be lost in the forest."

Ninsun, the goddess, queen of Egalmah, listened to her son. Then she clad herself to please, hung jewels on her breast, and bound her hair with gold. She climbed the many stairs to the altar of the sun. There she burned incense and raised her arms in prayer.

"Shamash, why have you stirred the heart of my son? Why

have you made him restless? If he is to challenge the dark one of the forest, the mighty Humbaba, give him your protection. From his going out to his coming back, give him your help."

Then she turned to Enkidu and promised him that he would become her adopted son if he protected Gilgamesh loyally and never left his side. As a pledge of this she hung an amulet around Enkidu's neck.

Gilgamesh and Enkidu armed themselves and departed from the city, the elders and counsellors crowding after them to the gates and shouting warnings and advice to the very last moment.

Then the journey began.

In three days they covered as much ground as an ordinary man would cover in two and a half months. They crossed seven mountains and then came to the gate of the forest, seventy-two cubits in height and twenty-four in width, fashioned in Nippur, the sacred city of Enlil.

Enkidu put his hand upon the gate to thrust it open. At once his hand was numb and paralyzed.

"Let us turn back," he cried.

But Gilgamesh persuaded him to have courage and reminded him of all the dangers they had already endured to get this far.

Together they passed through the gate and stood, awed, before a green mountain, a forest of mighty cedar that stretched in every direction. The rays of the sun scarcely penetrated to the ground at their feet.

Gilgamesh and Enkidu were struck dumb by its beauty, by its vastness, by its power.

The king dug a well before the sunset and scattered flour as an offering to the mountain, the forest, and the gods. The two then lay down to sleep.

In the night Gilgamesh had three dreams. In the first two, the mountain shook and rumbled and fell upon him until he was crushed. In the third, a light blazed out and a shining being stepped forward and pulled him out of the way of the falling mountain.

The next day the two companions penetrated deeper into the forest.

The second night Gilgamesh dreamed three dreams again. In the first two he and Enkidu were fighting hopelessly against wind and rain. In the third, everything became fire and all about them was turned to ash.

Frightened by the dream, Gilgamesh allowed himself to be persuaded by Enkidu to go down the mountain to the plain. But there he took his axe and felled a tree.

Far away in the depths of the forest, Humbaba, the watchman, heard the sound of the axe. Enraged, he came to see who had invaded his territory.

At his approach the sun was blotted out, and Gilgamesh fell into a trancelike sleep. Agitated on hearing the approach of the giant, Enkidu did everything in his power to rouse his companion.

At last Gilgamesh responded and girded on his armor. Enkidu tried to persuade him to flee back to the city while there was still time.

"No," Gilgamesh said; "he who leaves a challenge unresolved is never again at peace."

He stood his ground and waited for Humbaba.

But when Humbaba appeared, even he was filled with terror. Such size! Such strength! Such fearsome, deadly power!

Weeping, Gilgamesh called on Shamash for help, and Shamash loosed the winds. Bending to the god's breath, the huge trees swayed. The blast roared against Humbaba, pinning him back. He was unable to take another step forward.

Gilgamesh wielded his axe and felled another tree, and another, until seven cedars lay at the foot of the mountain and he stood directly before Humbaba.

Humbaba pleaded for mercy and offered to serve Gilgamesh and give him the run of the forest.

Gilgamesh was about to spare him when Enkidu spoke up and persuaded him not to trust the giant. And so three blows were struck. At the last one Humbaba was dead: the guardian of the cedar forest lay dead! Now there was nothing and no one to stop the destruction of the forest. Gilgamesh wielded his axe again and again. Enkidu cleared the roots. All the way to the banks of the Euphrates there was no more forest.

Proudly, Gilgamesh brought the head of Humbaba and laid it at the feet of Enlil, the god who had made him king. He laid the great palaces and temples and cities that he had built of cedar at the feet of the god who had made him king.

But the god was not pleased. The god was furious. The god raged at Gilgamesh that he had so betrayed his trust, that he had so misused his power.

"From now on the fire will sit where you sit, will eat the bread that you eat, will drink where you drink," he raged. "You will never be free of this deed you have done, and your name will be the name of a plunderer and not of a hero!"

As a punishment he decreed that one of them should die, and the choice fell on Enkidu.

Enkidu, fashioned of clay by the great goddess to be a worthy companion and friend for the king, lay ill and dying. Gilgamesh wept and rent his clothes, but nothing could stay the judgment of Enlil against the man who had encouraged Gilgamesh not to listen to the pleas of Humbaba for mercy and had helped to uproot the cedar trees so that the forests could not grow again.

⟡ COMMENT ⟡

The epic of Gilgamesh is based on fragments of ancient Sumerian material dating back to at least 3000 B.C.E. The most complete text we have was from the library of the Assyrian king Assurbanipal, which was destroyed in the sacking of Nineveh ca. 612 B.C.E. The stories might have been lost forever had not archaeologists in the nineteenth and twentieth centuries been working on the ruins of the great cities of the Middle East. Of the many fragments found, not all have been translated. The relevance of this story for our century, when the last great rain forests of the world are falling to the axe, is clear. Few will fail to see the parallel.

Gilgamesh is an epic hero. He may well have originated as a historic figure in ancient Uruk but, like the British King Arthur, he acquired legends around his name and has taken on a mythic, symbolic, archetypal role. He appears as part supernatural, part natural. His mother is said to be the goddess Ninsun, his father, a mortal man. Thus, he has a god's restless ambition for glory and a human mortality limiting the time in which to achieve it. We can identify with the frustrations of this situation; in a sense, we are all torn between the magnificent potential of our spiritual selves and the puny, time-burdened reality of our material selves. We are entrusted with power by our god, and more often than not we misuse it, leaving behind us nothing but despoilation and destruction.

Enkidu is a hero almost as great as Gilgamesh, fashioned by the god specifically to be his close companion. In this story he tries alternately to prevent Gilgamesh from going forward and to egg him on against his better judgment. We are reminded of the vari-

23

ous dialogues that go on within our own minds whenever we embark on any action—the dialogue between caution and daring, the dialogue between our higher and our lower selves.

Because this book is specifically concerned with tree myths and legends, I have not followed the Gilgamesh epic in further detail. To summarize, the death of Enkidu plunges Gilgamesh into such despair that he can no longer function as king. He leaves his country, goes into the wilderness, and after many trials and dangers finds the man he is seeking, the only mortal man who has been granted immortality by the gods. He finds out that a plant growing at the bottom of the ocean, if eaten, will give him the capacity to renew himself. He manages by great and heroic effort to obtain it and sets off home with it, but on the way a snake steals it from him. When he sees the snake slough its skin and slither away renewed, he becomes a broken man. In the end his great deeds come to nothing. He dies in the same manner as any peasant.

The plant that gives renewal is found at the bottom of the ocean—the primeval waters from which, many cultures believe, the first creations emerged. It is the ocean of God's consciousness, and in the great depths of our being where our spiritual selves dwell, we are still in harmony with it. This part of the story implies that only our spiritual selves from the great depths of the ocean can obtain immortality, and it is this search for our spiritual selves in the depths of the ocean of consciousness that ought to be our primary concern and the adventure we expend most personal effort upon. That Gilgamesh finds it only to lose it again emphasizes that finding is one thing but keeping is another. Often we have a transcendental experience that gives us briefly a knowledge of our higher selves, only to lose it again by carelessness when we return to the hurly-burly of everyday life.

In the forest sequence, Gilgamesh was looking for the immortality of fame, misunderstanding what true immortality meant. To achieve it he was prepared to ruin the environment. Only with Enkidu's death did he begin to understand where he was going wrong.

The most moving aspect of the story of Gilgamesh, to me, is that he is so nearly a truly spiritual hero but just misses. When Humbaba, the green man, the guardian of nature, asks that his life be spared and suggests that he could be the king's servant,

Gilgamesh, by listening to Enkidu's bad advice, turns down the opportunity to work *with* nature to the benefit of both man and tree. Almost too late, modern ecologists are advocating Humbaba's solution: that trees must be cut for human use, but not indiscriminately and not without careful planning and cooperation with nature itself.

We think back to the two sets of three dreams Gilgamesh had before he cut down the forest. The first set was of an earthquake— a natural disaster—in which he received the help and protection of shining beings, but the second set seems to be about the consequences if he himself causes the forest to disappear. We can see today how rainfall patterns change and fires take hold in forests that have been denuded by indiscriminate logging, as happened in Indonesia in 1991.

I have put this interpretation on the epic of Gilgamesh but do not necessarily believe it is the only possible interpretation. Recently I read Robert Temple's beautiful verse translation, *He Who Saw Everything*, and was very much impressed by it. Temple emphasizes the cosmic nature of the myth, associating it closely with the Babylonian interest in astronomy. In his version, Gilgamesh does not set out primarily to cut down the forest but to defeat the giant force Huwawa (Humbaba), who guards the cedar forest.

> *Gilgamesh spoke to Enkidu,*
> *Said to him:*
> *"In the forest terrible Huwawa lives.*
> *Let us, you and I, slay him,*
> *and banish all evil from the land."*
> *Robert Temple, Tablet iii*

The honor he seeks is to have conquered Huwawa himself. The cutting of the forest in Temple's version comes about as a side effect of the attack on Huwawa. This reading does not alter my belief that that part of the Gilgamesh story is about civilized, city-dwelling man destroying the natural environment because he fears it—because it is fierce and untamed and cannot be controlled.

Sources of myth

N. K. Sanders, *The Epic of Gilgamesh.*
Robert Temple, *He Who Saw Everything: A Verse Translation of the Epic of Gilgamesh.*

The Huluppa Tree

Sumerian

In the beginning, when everything was brought into being, when heaven had been separated from earth and the name of man was fixed, Enki, the god of wisdom, set sail through the tempest for the underworld, where Ereshkigal, the queen, reigned supreme. From their union the seed of a huluppa tree was planted on the banks of the Euphrates.

But a mighty south wind blew and pulled the tree up by its roots.

The young goddess Inanna, walking by the river, saw the tree being washed away downstream. She caught it and planted it in her sacred garden, believing that one day the wood of the tree would yield her a shining throne to sit upon and a shining bed to lie upon.

The years passed. The tree grew tall and thick, and Inanna wanted her throne and her bed. But three beings had made their home in the tree: a serpent who could not be charmed made its nest in the roots; an anzu bird built its nest in the branches; and Lilith, the woman of darkness, made her home in the trunk.

Inanna wept and called on her brother Utu to help her get rid of the intruders. But Utu, the valiant warrior, would not help his sister.

Then Inanna called upon her brother Gilgamesh, the hero of Uruk, to help her get rid of them. Gilgamesh buckled on his armor and took his great bronze axe into the garden. He struck the serpent who could not be charmed. The anzu bird flew away to the mountains, and Lilith fled to the wilderness.

Then Gilgamesh chopped down the tree, and from its trunk he carved a throne and a bed for his sister. From the roots of the tree she fashioned a pukka for her brother, and from the crown a mikku.

COMMENT

This Sumerian story dates from about 2000 B.C.E. Diane Wolkstein gives an interesting interpretation of it in *Inanna: Queen of Heaven and Earth* (cotranslated with Samuel Noah Kramer).

They see the three trespassers that live in the tree and prevent Inanna from having her throne and her bed as her "unacknowledged, unexpressed fears and desires." The serpent represents her sexuality, which "cannot be charmed"—that is, cannot be controlled. The anzu bird in Sumerian mythology "craves power and knowledge." In this context, the anzu bird could represent the craving for power and knowledge, which again cannot be controlled. Lilith appears often in the mythology of the Middle East but not often in Sumerian myth. She was supposed to be the first woman, fashioned from the clay at the same time as Adam. When she refused to lie down subserviently under him during the sex act, she became the symbol for the dark, aggressive side of woman's sexuality. In the Zohar, a fourteenth-century kabbalistic text, she is said to have dominion "over all instinctual, natural beings." Eve was made from Adam's rib to take her place—and to "know her place!"

So here we have Inanna's sexuality, her craving for power and knowledge, and her natural instincts—all unmanageable. Only when they have been brought under control can she have her throne (her power) and her bed (her mature womanliness).

This is an interesting suggestion, but I would have been happier had Inanna herself brought them under control. However, Gilgamesh is her brother, and they probably shared in the problem to be solved as much as in the solution to the problem. Utu, the thick-headed warrior, did not even see the problem. Gilgamesh, though showing definite tendencies toward wisdom and spirituality, has a long way to go before he is a mature and reliable hero-king.

Note that at the end Inanna and Gilgamesh both benefit from the tree—the tree that was born from the attraction of the opposite forces of Enki, the god of the higher consciousness, and Ereshkigul, the goddess of the dark, mysterious subconscious.

It is not known what a pukka or a mikku are, but Ms. Wolkstein suggests that they may be emblems of kingship, the rod and the ring seen in many Sumerian pictures. In that case, Gilgamesh takes from the tree much of what Inanna takes: mature control of himself.

Source of myth

Diane Wolkstein and Samuel Noah Kramer, *Inanna: Queen of Heaven and Earth*.

Mahavira

Indian/Jain

About 2,500 years ago a boy called Vardhamana grew up in a wealthy household with every comfort. But there was great restlessness in his soul for truth, and when he was thirty he left his home and went in search of it. As preparation, he sat under an asoka tree in the Shandavana park of the Jnatrikas in the outskirts of Kundapura for a year and a month. Then he embarked on a twelve-year quest for enlightenment, practicing extreme asceticism.

One day at Lollanga, near Nalenda, he was pressed to stay and build a hermitage by the Brahmin zamindar, Bahula, and to teach all who wanted to learn. He refused, saying he could not teach until he had learned truth and the path to nirvana by his own experience and vision. He would not stay in the house of Bahula but insisted on living in the forest. He told Bahula what he had already learned from nature.

"I have learned from the earth," he said, "patience and forbearance: from air to mix with all according to their nature; from fire the need to burn sin and evil thoughts, words, and deeds; from water and its slow action in wearing out the hardest rock by persistence that karma can be worn out by persistent effort; from the

sky, which keeps on the same despite changes underneath it, to be constant and to stick to one's own ideals in a changing world; from the sun to return good for evil just as he drinks the salt water of the ocean and gives in return fresh water in the shape of the rains, and also to treat all alike; from the moon to be indifferent to the waxing and waning of fortunes; from the clouds to be ever generous in giving all that one has; from the ocean to be indifferent to gain or loss just as it is indifferent to water flowing into it or being evaporated out of it; from the river to go on wandering until the goal is reached; from grass, life's inconstancy; from the tree, which gives shade even to the man who cuts it and even gives him its branch to make the handle of his axe to cut it with, magnanimity of spirit."

Then Vardhamana went to the dense forest and lived there alone for six months. During that time stories about him began to circulate. It was said that once he was sitting meditating cross-legged and motionless under a tree deep in the jungle. Some travellers passing by saw a tiger crouching beside him and drove it away with stones. When he ceased his meditation, they told him of the danger he had been in, and he smiled and said he had been in no danger from his brother. When the travellers left, they looked back and saw that the tiger was lying beside him again.

After the forest sojourn he taught the principles of nonviolence wherever he went. "Self-control is essential for spiritual development," he said in reply to being asked why he did not hit back when attacked. "Meet hate with love, violence with nonviolence, greed by gift, untruth by truth."

In the dangerous Ladha country he was set upon by the fierce dogs of the hunters. He stood his ground. "You poor things," he said, "neither your barkings nor your bites will affect me. They will only add to your karma. The pity of it is that you do not do it of yourselves but are set on by your masters."

As his reputation as a holy man grew, some who would be his disciples pleaded with him to teach them miraculous powers: the ability to make oneself as small as an atom, as big as a universe, as light as a feather, or as heavy as the earth; the capacity to enter dead bodies, make oneself invisible, attract any person by the strength of one's irresistible will, or win over people and lord it over them to get whatever one wants. But he refused, saying,

"These are toys which fasten man to material things and interfere with his salvation. They have no spiritual value. So, I shall not teach you these things, as no teacher ought to teach things not conducive to salvation."

After twelve years of wandering, of meditating, of enduring incredible hardships from privation and at the hands of jealous and antagonistic people who felt threatened by his uncompromising purity, he again came to rest under a tree, this time under a sal tree in a field on the banks of a river, and there at last found what he had been seeking.

In a moment of magnificent revelation he possessed infinite knowledge and nirvana. But in his compassion for suffering humanity he stayed to help and teach others to find the path. Under the name of Mahavira he taught that "the infinite joy of nirvana lies along a narrow razor's edge beset with sorrow and penance" and not in "endless prayers and ceremonies."

He annoyed many people by preaching against the caste system.

"The whole creation consists of only two main castes," he said, "the living and the intelligent, and the nonliving and unintelligent matter."

"Are there no castes among the living?" he was asked.

"Oh yes, there are four castes," he replied, "but not the ones you proclaim. The real castes are the devas, or residents of the heavens; the human beings; the animal, vegetable, and mineral kingdoms; and the demons, or denizens of hells. All human beings belong to one caste and are all capable of perfection by working out their karma."

"Do you think women can be imparted spiritual knowledge equally with men?" he was asked.

"Oh yes," said Mahavira. "Women differ from men to some extent in their bodies, to a much lesser extent in their minds, to a still lesser extent in their egos, and not at all in their souls."

He taught that each person is responsible for working out his or her own salvation.

"Alone a man is born, alone he dies, alone he rises to a higher state by his own exertions, alone he falls to a lower state by his own wicked acts." At another time he said, "The noise of the marketplace and your own babbling will drown the silence of all the worlds. In the silence of meditation we are like the roads at night, listening to the foot-falls of truth." And again, "Truth raises against itself the storm that scatters its seed broadcast."

His sermons became famous. Many thousands of seekers sat at his feet and learned by question and answer and by simply being in his presence.

~~ COMMENT ~~

It is not possible in this short account to give all the teachings of Mahavira of the Jains. This is a book about trees, and it is no co-incidence that Buddha reached enlightenment under a tree, and the young Vardhamana made his commitment to begin his quest for truth under a tree and completed it under a tree.

In every major Hindu temple there is a sacred tree, for the tree is rooted in earth and reaches to heaven. The tree is of the natural world yet lends itself easily to the symbolism of the supernatural. In the shade provided by it against the scorching sun of India, moments of peace can be found. Shaded from the dazzling of the material world, we can see the more subtle and profound visions of the spiritual world.

The incident of the tiger I see as a comment on the oneness of all things. When we are so still in body and mind that we have become one with stone and tree and animal, the tiger feels no threat and lies beside the sage as much at peace as the sage is with himself.

The incident of the dogs I see as a comment on wars in which the ordinary soldier has no quarrel with his neighbor but is ordered to attack by the politicians and generals for their own purposes. Sadly, this will not free him from bearing the responsibility for his actions in future lives.

The miraculous powers condemned by Mahavira are still a temptation to the unenlightened today. Many magazine advertisements purport to be about enlightened matters but offer the readers easy ways to obtain their every wish by magical means. "Rub this Buddha's stomach," I read once, "and chant these words a thousand times and you will get the new car you want." Christ and Buddha and all the mighty beings of light must often despair at humanity's persistent misunderstanding of their message!

A. S. P. Ayyap's most interesting book, *Famous Tales of Ind*, tells of many other instances of enlightenment being received under trees. One is of the woman sage Kavundi, who sat under an asoka tree in the Jain temple in Kaundapalli. In concentrating on the All-Knowing she saw him represented as standing in unbroken serenity under three umbrellas, one over the other, symbolizing the three evils of the body, mind, and ego that have to be pierced before he can be reached.

Source of myth

A. S. P. Ayyap, *Famous Tales of Ind*.

The Bodhi Tree

Indian/Buddhist

Siddhartha Gautama was born into a wealthy and noble family in Nepal ca. 566 B.C.E. His mother had dreamed that a great and holy man was about to be born from her body. She clutched the branches of two blossoming trees as her labor started and drew strength and energy from them as she gave birth. Soon after birth the infant took seven steps in each cardinal direction; then, pointing to heaven with one hand and to the earth with the other, proclaimed that he had come to abolish suffering.

His mother died seven days after he was born, and he was brought up by his aunt. His father saw to it that he led a life of luxury and comfort, protected from all hardships and disturbing sights. He wanted his son to inherit his wealth and power and tried to steer him away from the religious vocation that seemed to be intended for him by the circumstances surrounding his birth.

At sixteen Siddhartha was married, but at twenty-nine he was shaken out of his comfortable acceptance of life by four confrontations. One was with an old and decrepit man, slobbering, incontinent, and gibbering; another with a young man wasting away with a dreadful disease; the third with a rotting corpse; and the fourth with a strong, calm monk pursuing a life of contemplation. He was no longer satisfied with his rich food and comfortable life

and the impermanence of the luxury he enjoyed. The fear that what he had seen in the first three encounters might become his own fate spoiled those pleasures for him. He decided to emulate the monk and set off to study with one sage after another, ceaselessly seeking the answer to a question that now obsessed him: how to overcome the fear of age, suffering, and death.

The teachers he found did not satisfy Siddhartha. For a while he chose to live a life of extreme asceticism, but he grew so weak he almost died. His fear was as strong as ever. No answer had come to his questioning even though he had renounced the distraction of every worldly pleasure and comfort.

He decided extreme asceticism would not give him the answer and allowed himself some food. Believing he had failed and was no longer worth following, his five companions left him.

At Bodh-Gaya he sat under a tree and did not move from there for forty-nine days.

Time passed and did not pass.

He could feel the great tree drawing nourishment and energy from the earth. He could feel it drawing nourishment and energy from the air and the sun. He began to feel the same energy pumping in his heart. He began to feel that there was no distinction between the tree and himself. He was the tree. The tree was him. The earth and the sky were also part of the tree and hence of him.

When his companions came that way again, they found him so shining and radiant they could hardly look at him directly.

"What has happened?" they asked.

But he did not reply.

How could he possibly explain in words the experience that had given him the key to the question that had troubled him so deeply for so long? He could have said: "There is no distinction. There is no suffering once one experiences the wholeness of things. There is only suffering if we think in terms of separation: I and Thou, this and that, before and after, here and there. There is only suffering if we desire what we think is outside ourselves, not realizing that we have everything because everything is contained within the 'I.' The infant born and the old man dying are part of one experience and there should be no rejoicing for the one and mourning for the other. What is, is." These things, if he had said them, would have gone some way to explaining what he had learned, but not far enough. To know in part is to know nothing.

He took a leaf from the tree and looked at it. In it was the whole essence of the tree. In it was the essence of the universe. He held it out to his disciples. They saw it glowing with the same radiance that he saw.

At the age of thirty-five, as age is reckoned on earth, Siddhartha Gautama became an "Awakened One," a Buddha, and knew that he would be freed from the Wheel of Becoming, the ceaselessly turning wheel of time, because he had learned how to overcome suffering. Nirvana was his—being without motion, being without change, being that was complete, for there was nothing that it was not.

His companions pleaded with him to share with them something of what he had learned, and at last he stood up and walked with them. He set in motion the wheel of learning. He passed from place to place gathering disciples until he died at the age of eighty, so perfect a being that he left no earthly remains but only the inspiration of his word.

❧ COMMENT ❧

It seems not to be enough that the symbol of the tree as the growing center of consciousness and source of enlightenment is given to us in the story of the Buddha. Generations of men and women have wanted to know exactly where the physical tree was under which Buddha sat, and what kind of tree it was—as though either of these questions is of any significance. Some traditions say the tree was a fig tree, others that it was a pipal, others that it was a banyan. It is known most universally as the Bodhi tree.

"The Buddhist legends," writes Roger Cook in his book *The Tree of Life* (pp. 21-22), "tell how the Buddha, having finally arrived at a thorough understanding of the finite limitations and conditions of existence, resolved to transcend them through renunciation. He resolved that, though his bones would waste away and his blood dry up, he would not leave his seat beneath the sacred banyan tree until he had successfully transcended the conditions of existence and broken through to an immediate realization of the Ultimate and Unconditional Truth (Bodhi)." During the forty-nine days he sat under the tree, fearsome and dark illusions beset him from every side, but he "remained immovably fixed at the center; spiritually, he was one with the axis of the universe; symbolically he had climbed the Cosmic Tree and was viewing the antics of Kama-Mara (the demonic lord of the cosmic process) from another plane." Often in Buddhist texts the Bodhi tree rather than Buddha himself "is referred to as the 'Great Awakener.'"

According to *The Rider Encyclopaedia of Eastern Philosophy and Religion* (p. 40) there is still today a descendant of the tree under which Siddhartha meditated beside the Mahabodhi temple in Bodh-Gaya. The original tree is said to have been destroyed in the seventh century by the Bengali king Shashanka. A shoot still grew but was destroyed in a storm in 1876. The tree venerated today is believed to be descended from a shoot of the original tree that was taken to Ceylon in the third century B.C.E.

If a pilgrimage to the Bodhi tree will open up your heart and help create the mood to understand the Buddha's teachings, by all means make the pilgrimage. But to my mind the experience of one man cannot be repeated by following literally in his steps. Each of us has a "Bodhi tree" waiting for us—and it may be that it is in our own back garden.

Siddhartha's followers, like the followers of Christ, wrote down the master's words, and the piles of words grew and grew. Scholars and acolytes debated the meaning of the Four Noble Truths: the Truth of Suffering (that existence is characterized by suffering), the Truth of the Origin of Suffering (craving and desire for something we think we do not have), the Truth of the Cessation of Suffering (the elimination of craving), and the Truth of the Path that leads to the Cessation of Suffering (the Eightfold Path of perfect view, perfect resolve, perfect thought, perfect speech, perfect action, perfect livelihood, perfect effort, and perfect concentration).

Monasteries sprang up all over India, Tibet, China, Burma, and Japan. The teaching spread to the West—to Europe and to America. But no number of words written or spoken can ever give us completely what the Buddha experienced under that Bodhi tree. We have to win our own radiance. We have to achieve our own enlightenment, and there is no sure and common way to do it. That is at once our despair and our hope.

Joseph Campbell, in *The Mythic Image* (pp. 11, 194, 195), makes an interesting comparison between the tree of knowledge of good and evil in the garden of Eden, where the approach to the tree and eating of the fruit cause man and woman to be sunk deep into the mire of fear, lust, and death, and the Bodhi tree where Buddha reaches a knowledge of good and evil that can save men and women from slavery to fear, lust, and death. In both cases the tempter is present. Adam and Eve succumb; Buddha does not. Perhaps the cross, the rough-hewn tree, rather than the original tree in the garden of Eden, is a better comparison for the Bodhi tree. On this tree Christ accepts his destiny. Tempters point out that he could leap down and avoid suffering if he used his miraculous powers. The enlightened one, the son of God, refuses, knowing that his example of selfless acceptance of truth, his transcendence of fear and worldly ambition is crucial to his message. It is also significant in this connection that both Buddha and Christ suffer during the experience of attaining their goal: Buddha during forty-nine days on the Bardo planes, and Christ physically and no doubt mentally and emotionally. In both cases mind and ego are transcended through suffering. The analogy cannot be pushed too far because there are major differences, but the similarity is clear to one who reflects on both events. Roger Cook carries the influence of the mythic symbol further by reminding us that the Scandinavian god Odin hung, suffering, for nine days on the great cosmic tree Yggdrasil to achieve wisdom.

The implication for us may well be that the tree will not give us wisdom if we take thoughtlessly and selfishly of its bounty, but only if we join our nature to its own and identify with its slow and painstaking growth process.

Sources of myth
The Rider Encyclopaedia of Eastern Philosophy and Religion.
Roger Cook, *The Tree of Life.*
Joseph Campbell, *The Mythic Image.*

The Old Tree

Chinese

A carpenter and his apprentice passed an old tree next to an earth-altar.

"What a magnificent tree," said the apprentice. "Look at its girth. It must be of a very great age."

"It is certainly old," said the carpenter, "but it is useless. The wood is no good for building ships or for making tools."

That night the old tree appeared to the carpenter in a dream and complained that he had compared him unfairly to other trees that bore fruit or had hard wood suitable for ship-building or tool-making. "Those trees," he said, "have a very short span of life. Their fruit is picked, their twigs broken. Woodmen are constantly chopping at them and they hardly reach any age at all. Look at me! Do you think I would have reached this age had I been considered useful by men? Do you think I am doing nothing useful? Yet I am growing beside this earth-altar."

In the morning the carpenter told his apprentice that the great old tree should be respected, for had it not grown to a great age, and was it not growing beside an earth-altar?

~ COMMENT ~

The carpenter after his dream understood "that each of us has a unique task of self-realization. Although many human problems are similar, they are never identical. All pine trees are very much alike (otherwise we should not recognize them as pines), yet none is exactly the same as another. Because of these factors of sameness and difference, it is difficult to summarize the infinite variations of the process of individuation. The fact is that each person has to do something different, something that is uniquely his own" (Carl G. Jung, *Man and His Symbols,* p. 164).

The seed of a pine "contains the whole future tree in latent form; but each seed falls at a certain time onto a particular place, in which there are a number of special features. . . . The latent totality of the pine in the seed reacts to these circumstances by avoiding the stones and inclining toward the sun, with the result that the tree's growth is shaped. Thus an individual pine slowly comes into existence, constituting the fulfillment of its totality, its emergence into the realm of reality" (Carl G. Jung, *Man and His Symbols,* p. 162).

We cannot dictate how another person must reach fulfillment, for our circumstances are never the same. Without any outward or visible sign of "useful achievement" one may still reach the realization of one's higher self and contribute, by one's very presence, to the power and sanctity of an earth-altar, which without that presence might have been no more than a forgotten and unnoticed slab of stone.

One might also, by one's calm and venerable acceptance of one's situation and by one's quiet rootedness in earth and aspiration toward heaven, be an example to others and provide a haven of rest for restless and unhappy people that will help them to renew their journey with fresh hope and vigor.

Source of myth
    Carl G. Jung, *Man and His Symbols,* quoting a story by Chuang-Tzu,
    "The Chinese Sage."

Isis and the Tamarisk Tree

Egyptian

Atum the mighty, the most ancient sun-god, venerated before all others, produced from himself Shu, the god of light and air, and Tefnut, the goddess of water, the male and female progenitors of the sky goddess Nut and the earth god Geb, who in turn were the parents of the sacred four: Osiris, Isis, Set, and Nepthys.

Osiris and Isis, brother and sister, husband and wife, ruled as king and queen in the early days, and with their wisdom and strength brought order and justice to the wild and barbaric lands beside the Nile. They taught with words and music alone, finding no call for weapons.

Their brother, Set, however, was jealous of their power and of their success and conspired with seventy-two companions and the Queen of Nubia to bring about their destruction.

He ordered a chest to be made of the finest Nubian ebony wood, decorated and inlaid with ivory, gold, and precious stones. He was careful to have it made to the exact measurements of his brother Osiris.

One evening, during a feast of celebration, he showed off the magnificent chest and said he would give it to whomsoever it would fit. Many tried it for size, but none could fit into it comfort-

ably until Osiris climbed inside. Immediately Set slammed shut the lid and drew the bolt while some of his seventy-two fellow conspirators rushed forward with vats of boiling lead and poured it over the chest and others held back the shocked and horrified Isis.

Triumphantly, Set had the chest removed and thrown into the mouth of the river near Tanis in the Nile Delta. From thence it was pushed out into the Great Green Ocean by the force of the inundation.

Currents bore it to the shore near Byblos, where it was washed up on the beach, its sharp edges cutting into the trunk of a tamarisk sapling. The young tree took strength from the buried god, and the wound healed over the leaden chest, the trunk soon closing over so completely that the box was lost to sight. Never before had a tamarisk grown to such a width or such a height. Never before had its flowers hung so profusely and for so long.

Local people began to remark on the extraordinary tree, and soon travellers came from far and wide to see it.

The story of its miraculous growth reached the king of the country and his queen, Astarte, and workmen were sent to cut the tree down and bring it to the palace. There it was installed as the central column of a great hall.

Meanwhile, a desperate Isis, at last released by her captors, went in search of her husband's body, anxious to perform the correct funeral rituals so that his soul might enter the Duat, the Land beyond Death.

Some children heard her weeping on the banks of the river and told her how they had seen the chest washed out to sea. Others told her they had seen it drifting east, and by dint of persistent questioning and travelling she traced it along the eastern coast of the Mediterranean Sea.

When she reached the city of Byblos, she heard the tale of the miraculous tamarisk tree and how it was now a column in the palace of the king.

She disguised herself as an old woman, and when the queen's handmaidens came down to the water to bathe, she spoke to them. When they returned to the palace, the scent of the goddess was so strong upon them that the queen questioned them. They told her they did not know where the scent had come from, only that they had been speaking to a strange old lady down by the water's edge. The queen ordered her to be fetched, and suspecting that she was a wise woman capable of healing magic, she employed her as nurse to her ailing son.

Isis remained at the palace, and each day the boy seemed to be growing stronger and healthier. All would have been well had the handmaidens not reported the strange behavior of the woman to the queen.

"Each night," they said, "she locks herself and the boy into the great hall with the tamarisk column. We have listened at the door and all we can hear is the twittering of a bird."

The next day the queen hid herself in the hall so that when Isis came to lock the doors, the queen was inside the hall with her. She saw the old woman make a fire and lay the young prince on top of it. While he was lying there surrounded by flames, the old woman transformed herself into a swallow and flew round and round the tamarisk column.

Horrified, the queen rushed out and snatched her son from the flames, shouting abuse at the old woman for being a wicked necromancer and promising her severe punishment.

But suddenly the swallow was transformed into the huge and towering figure of the goddess Isis, who berated the queen for having spoiled the spell she was weaving on the child to make him immortal.

The queen fell on her knees, weeping and begging forgiveness.

Isis demanded that the column be split open.

It was done. And the coffin of Osiris was revealed.

Isis left the wood of the tamarisk tree with the king and the queen, for the tree had held the body of a god and was worthy to be venerated. But she took the coffin back with her to Egypt.

There she secretly opened it. In the guise of a hawk, she hovered over it, beating her wings to drive air into her dead husband's lungs. For a brief moment her beloved lived again, and in that moment he impregnated her with the seed of their son Horus.

While Isis was away in the marshes giving birth, Set found the coffin of Osiris, his body within still uncorrupted. Furiously, he hauled him out and chopped his body into fourteen pieces, scattering the pieces all over Egypt.

How Isis, mourning, sought out the pieces of her husband one

47

by one and gave them burial, and how her son Horus avenged his father's murder is another story.

COMMENT

Many different versions of this story are told. George Hart describes the tree as a heath tree, but several other authors, including Roger Lancelyn Green and M. V. Seton-Williams, call it a tamarisk tree.

George Hart points out that the first version of the story is found late, in Plutarch during the first century A.D., but it may well be based on older versions now lost. That Osiris has been associated with a sacred tree since very ancient times suggests that Plutarch was right—this is a very old legend. At Herakleopolis, the place venerated as the tomb of Osiris is under a sacred tree, and in one of the chapels at Karnak, Osiris is associated with a sacred persea tree. He is certainly known as a god of renewal, regeneration, even resurrection. In paintings he is represented with black skin to indicate the rich fertile silt of the inundation that gives life to the lands along the Nile, or with green skin to represent the growth of plants. In tombs, wooden frames in the shape of his body are filled with earth and planted with barley seed to represent the idea that the seeds will germinate in the tomb as the soul will germinate and grow beyond death. In the tomb of Yuya and Thuya the barley had grown eight inches tall.

Osiris is sometimes described as the twin of Ra, because Ra is ruler of this world and Osiris is ruler of the otherworld. He was a great and just king when he was alive and is a great and just king still. Before him the hearts of the deceased are weighed against the feather of truth, and his judgment decides their fate.

It is no accident that in this story his coffin is enclosed in a tree and the tree subsequently grows miraculously. Through his death, all growing things of the earth regenerate. The seed "dies" and is buried so that the new corn may spring up and nourish the people of the earth. That symbol is used again and again in practically every religion. The god is sacrificed to bring life and renewal to his people. "Unless ye be born again . . ."

Another universal theme in this story is the duality of good and evil, light and dark, Cain and Abel, Osiris and Set, and the eternal conflict between them—evil apparently winning only to lose in the end. Osiris as king of the otherworld is far more powerful than he was as an earthly king.

It's often puzzling in these legends that the gods and goddesses are not as all-powerful as we might expect. Isis does not see at once where the coffin is, nor does she—once she knows—go straight for it and take it back. She disguises herself as an old woman and tricks her way into the palace like any ordinary mortal. She secretly practices magic rituals. She transforms herself into a swallow and flies helplessly around her entombed lover, crying piteously. Why?

Perhaps the gods we encounter in these legends—though a different order of being from us—are not yet of the highest. Perhaps they are related more to the angels and archangels of the Christian, Jewish, and Islamic traditions or to the bodhisattvas of the Buddhist tradition than to the Ultimate One, the Supreme Being everyone is seeking and no one can describe. They have trials and difficulties to overcome as we do. They too are striving to progress upward as are we. Isis and Osiris, having allowed themselves to be tricked, must pay for it and work their passage to greater awareness, greater wisdom. If overcoming mistakes is too easy, nothing is learned or gained.

Besides—if we have a measure of free will—it is important that we are not interfered with too arbitrarily and too often by supernatural forces. The queen must invite Isis into her life. A healer I know who works with spirit helpers says that if you want healing you must ask for it, because any interference from them without invitation would be a violation of your basic right to free will.

Another factor is that historically in the ancient world, and indeed in legends generally, a king and queen are considered divine. The tamarisk is in the palace of the king and cannot be summarily seized—not even by a goddess. You may wonder why there are so many kings and queens, princes and princesses in myths and legends. I am sure the titles are symbolic and serve to isolate the protagonist from the mass of ordinary people in one sense, even while making him or her representative of them in another. The protagonist in the story is important and special—elevated from the crowd for us all to see—and yet universally representative.

In this story the queen is working out a problem of her own.

Isis and she are linked. Her child is wasting away, which indicates symbolically that something is wrong in the palace, or the kingdom, or the mother's heart. The child cannot be healed by natural means. The queen smells and recognizes the scent of a goddess. She is not enlightened enough to recognize the old woman as Isis herself, but she is enlightened enough to know that the disguised Isis is no ordinary woman and to believe that only through supernatural means can the malaise be lifted. She trusts the old wise woman with her son but is easily turned from her trust by the ignorant tattling of her servants. She spies on the old woman; she cannot see that her son is not burning in the fire but mistakes it for natural fire and loses all her faith.

Isis confronts her at this moment. When we are at our lowest, in the "dark night of the soul," we are at our most vulnerable for change and transformation and most ready for transcendental revelation. The queen sees Isis in her full glory and regrets having lost faith. But the moment has passed. Her son must stay mortal because of her loss of faith, though he is now well and strong. Isis gets her husband back—but also not quite as she would have wished.

Sources of myth

George Hart, *A Dictionary of Egyptian Gods and Goddesses.*
Roger Lancelyn Green, *Tales of Ancient Egypt.*
M. V. Seton-Williams, *Egyptian Legends and Stories.*

The Two Brothers

Egyptian

There were once two brothers, orphans. The elder was Anpu and the younger Bata. The younger lived with the elder as though with a father and spent his days working in the fields and with the cattle to make his brother prosperous. There was great love between them.

One day when the two were working together in the fields, Anpu sent Bata back, to the house to fetch more grain for planting.

As the younger brother heaved five sacks of grain onto his back the wife of Anpu was observing him.

"You are strong," she said, "and virile. I desire you. Come to my chamber and make love to me."

But Bata was shocked and angry, and he refused.

He strode off back to the fields with the bags of grain and said nothing to his brother.

That night as usual Anpu returned home earlier than Bata. He found his wife weeping and her garments torn.

"It was your brother," she said. "He found me alone when he came for the grain, and he tried to rape me."

Anpu could hardly believe her because the young man had

proved to be so exemplary in every way up to this time. But his wife wept louder and swore she would kill herself rather than face Bata again.

When Bata was driving the cows into the barn, the first one to cross the threshold said to him, "Beware, your brother is angry and is behind the door with a knife ready to kill you." Bata could not believe it, but when the second cow and the third also warned him he turned and fled.

Anpu pursued him. The god Harmarchis, looking down, saw the trouble one of his favorites was in and placed a channel of water full of crocodiles between the two brothers. Then, safe on the other side, Bata managed to convince Anpu that he had been falsely accused. He told him what had really happened. Anpu asked his forgiveness at once and promised to punish his wife. He pleaded for his brother to return.

But Bata said he could no longer live with a brother who so easily believed such ill of him. He declared that he was going away, far away, to live in the land of the acacias.

"What I will do," he said, "is leave you a sign so that you will always know how it fares with me. I will house one part of my soul in the top of an acacia tree, and if I die, the beer you drink will go cloudy. Then you must come looking for me. Find my soul and put it in a cup of water. In that way it will revive, and I, Bata, will live again."

So the brothers parted.

Many years went by. In the land of the acacias, Bata built a great house for his body, but one part of his soul remained in the topmost flowers of a particularly tall acacia tree.

One day the gods were walking in the acacia grove and remarked that Bata was alone.

"Let us give him a companion," they said, and they created a beautiful woman for him. Khnum fashioned her of clay on his potter's wheel, and the others breathed life into her. They forgot, however, to pay enough attention to her heart.

The goddess Hathor saw the woman and forecast that she would meet a sharp death.

Bata was pleased with his wife, and they lived happily together for a time. He told her everything about himself, including the secret of where the vital part of his soul rested in the acacia flowers. He warned her never to go near the river, because she was so beautiful he believed that Hapi, the river god, would want to take her for his own.

Needless to say, because it was forbidden, she wanted more than anything to walk by the river. One day when he was away from home, she stood on the riverbank and looked at her reflection in the water. As Bata had feared, Hapi desired her and reached up his watery arms to seize her. She drew back at once, but not before he had ripped off a lock of her hair.

The lock was born away on the current until it came to Mennefer, where the pharaoh lived. The beautiful scent of it permeated his clothes when they were washed in the waters of the river. For a long while the mystery of why the clothes had such a sweet odor could not be solved. One day, a priest of Ptah noticed the lock of hair in the water and declared that such a lock could only have come from the daughter of a god.

Then Pharaoh set about trying to trace the owner of the lock of hair and sent out messengers throughout the country. At last, word came that a woman living in an acacia grove was undoubtedly the owner of the lock. Soldiers were sent to escort her to the king, but Bata killed them.

Then Pharaoh sent sweet-talking courtiers, who spoke to the woman when she was alone and persuaded her to leave her husband and the rough and lonely life of the acacia grove for the rich and luxurious life of the court.

She went secretly and willingly, and she became the favorite of the king.

She was so pleased with her new life that she feared Bata would come and claim her back. She told the king that Bata could be killed if the tree that housed his soul was chopped down and burned.

Pharaoh at once dispatched soldiers to destroy the tree.

Bata, in his house a distance away, died as the tree was consumed by the flames.

Anpu, lifting his mug of beer to his lips, found that it was cloudy.

He set off in search of his brother and found his corpse in the house among the acacia trees. Remembering the instructions he had been given, he searched everywhere for the soul. Almost in despair, after three long years, he was about to turn for home when he noticed an acacia seed on the ground. He placed it in a cup of water, and almost immediately the body of his brother began to revive. Bata told Anpu what had happened and declared that before the sun rose his soul would enter the body of a magnificent bull. Anpu must take this bull to Pharaoh, and the king would handsomely reward him.

This Anpu did, and Bata in the form of a bull came to live in Men-nefer near his wife. Anpu returned home a rich and honored man.

The king's favorite wife chanced to be alone one day with the bull and was horrified when it spoke and told her that it was Bata. She went to the king at once and set about pleasing him more than she had ever pleased him before. When she could see he desired her more than he ever had, she drew back and asked for a boon.

"Anything," he vowed.

She desired to eat the heart of the bull Anpu had brought to the palace, she said. The king tried to dissuade her, but he could not go back on his oath and she would not change her mind. The beautiful bull was killed and the heart was brought to the pharaoh's favorite. But as the servants carried it through the main gateway two drops of blood fell from it and landed one on each side of the great pylon. Instantly, two miraculous persea trees sprang up and gave shade to all who entered the palace.

Convinced that she was now truly free of her former husband, the young woman walked between the persea trees, but in their rustling she fancied she heard Bata's voice and knew that she had failed to destroy him once again.

She tricked her husband into promising her anything she desired. This time she demanded that the persea trees be cut down and burned.

Again, regretfully, Pharaoh ordered her whim to be carried out, and she, watching the trees as they were chopped to pieces, laughed aloud. As she laughed a tiny chip of wood flew into her open mouth, and she swallowed it.

Nine months later she gave birth to a prince, who in the fullness of time became Pharaoh of Egypt.

When he was crowned he made a public pronouncement that he was indeed Bata himself and that he had been systematically wronged by the woman who was once his wife but was now his mother. She was executed, and Bata ruled Egypt for many years. His brother Anpu was his right-hand man.

COMMENT

Whatever story is told, it seems that the ancient Egyptians have told it already. The theme of the faithless wife who entices a young man to her chamber and then, when he refuses to come, cries "rape" and tries to bring about his death is not uncommon in myth and legend.

In "The Limbless One," the Buddhist story of Caurangipa told in *Masters of Enchantment* and retold in my book *Crystal Legends,* the scorned wife demands that the limbs of the young man be cut off and that he be thrown into the forest to die. He does not die but masters the art of meditation and becomes a mahasiddha, an enlightened one.

Then there is the story of Joseph and Potiphar's wife in the Bible (Genesis 39), in which the woman's evil intentions go wrong and the noble youth who refuses her reaps a handsome reward.

In both cases the young man is a good person and well favored. He is offered temptation. He resists. The woman frames him by tearing her clothes and shouting rape. He is punished, but justice triumphs in the end. Joseph is flung into prison after the false accusations of his master's wife, but he interprets Pharaoh's dreams while he is in prison and becomes a rich and honored official in Pharaoh's administration in the end. Bata becomes Pharaoh himself.

The theme of the wife who is especially fashioned by the gods to be a companion for a lonely man can be found in more than one story. Eve is made from Adam's rib in Eden and causes his downfall by eating the forbidden fruit and persuading him to do likewise. Bloddeud, in the ancient Celtic legend told in *The Mabinogion,* is fashioned of flowers by the gods to be the wife of Llew Llaw Gyffes, who had been cursed by his mother, the goddess Arianrhod, so that he could not have a wife born of woman. Like Bata's wife, Bloddeud is beautiful but amoral. She has the outward and visible form of a woman but not the heart. In fact, she is so two-dimensional that one wonders whether she is meant not to be a separate being at all but only one part of a whole person. These are myths, after all, not reports of actual events—and in myth the various aspects of one person are often given separate identities so that the point can be made.

The Celtic Llew Llaw Gyffes, like Bata, can be killed only in a very specific and elaborate way. The wife finds this out, tells the rival, has him killed, and prepares to live happily ever after with the murderer. But in both cases the wronged husband does not actually die. He is transformed: Llew Llaw Gyffes into a wounded eagle surviving in the top of an oak tree, and Bata into a bull and then into a persea tree. Thus both are able to come through the experience and rule a country (that is, themselves) nobly and well. Through adversity and their handling of it they have both found their higher selves. Through transformation, through dying to this world, they are born again.

Another husband whose wife finds out his fatal weak spot and uses it for his destruction is Samson, whose name means "like the sun" (Judges 16). Delilah wheedles his secret out of him and has his hair shorn so that his enemies may blind him, mock him, and keep him captive. The story seems to be headed for a sad ending, except that the sacrificial nobility of Samson as he pulls the building down on his enemies and himself changes it once more into a story of the triumph of a noble soul, destined for great things, tried and tested and proved worthy against all the odds.

The theme of the soul kept outside the body in an apparently safe place while the body goes on about its everyday business is also not uncommon in myths and fairy stories. It is based on a very strong belief that the body and the soul are two separate entities and that one can survive without the other. The belief shared by so many great religions in the existence of a life after bodily death is based on this concept, as are no doubt the West Indian and West African voodoo practices.

Bata puts part of his soul in the acacia tree. The ancient Egyptians believed that the person consisted of nine different parts, each capable of separate identity and capable of functioning separately. "*Ka* was a form that we today might call the astral body, the ba one stage more removed from the physical, the soul of the individual. The *akh* or *khu* was more abstract still, the eternal essence of the spirit, the highest form of being. To the ancient Egyptians, the *name*, the *shadow*, the *intelligence*, the *heart*, the *power of will*—all had their own energy and were, in a mysterious sense we don't quite understand, capable of being separate entities after death" (Moyra Caldecott, *Daughter of Amun*, p. 364). Exactly what part of himself Bata put in the acacia tree I am not sure, but it was probably the spirit equivalent of the heart. The wife asks to eat the heart of the bull when she discovers it is Bata.

Once we accept the separate existence of a nonphysical part of ourselves, it is not difficult to accept that that part can appear in any physical form it likes—as a bull or as a tree. The bull possibly represents the strong, fierce, dangerous, masculine, animal part of Bata; the tree, the stable, beautiful, more ethereal side, creating shade and comfort for others, nonthreatening. After all, on this long journey of self-discovery and adventure, only one tiny chip is used to create the new man. Looking back on a long life, one often wonders what it was all about when only one or two events in it seem seminal, but of course all of it has played a role in keeping the vital spark—the growing, adventuring, developing shoot—nourished and protected.

Impregnation of a woman by mouth rather than by the usual method is also not an uncommon theme. It occurs in the story of Ceridwen and Taliesin in the Welsh *Mabinogion*. Alarmed that the boy Gwion has swallowed three drops of the extraordinarily potent mixture she has been brewing in her cauldron, which will give him total knowledge of past, present, and future, Ceridwen pursues him. He changes into a hare, but she pursues him as a hound. He dives into the river and changes into a fish, but she is after him as an otter. He leaps and transforms into a bird, but she flies over him as a hawk. Desperately he becomes a grain of wheat, and quickly, as a hen, she pecks him up and swallows him. Nine months later he is born. That is, the ordinary village lad who sucked the three potent drops off his fingers is reborn through Ceridwen as the greatest poet and prophet the world has ever known—Taliesin.

The appearance and repeated use of these themes in many cultures does not necessarily imply that these cultures were in physical contact with one another. These themes symbolize something important for us, something that touches the part of us that is not fashioned by our environment or our culture but by our journey through eternity.

Why are there two brothers in this story? Perhaps one represents ordinary life whereas the other represents the questing soul. The younger needs the elder to help him; he cannot achieve what he wants to achieve by himself. In many myths, mortal men are called upon to enter the otherworld and do some favor or service for the gods. Cuchulain in Irish myth and Pwyll in Welsh myth are both taken into the otherworld to fight a battle against the enemy of the god. The implication is that the level or realm in which the soul of the protagonist operates is half in the physical and half in the spiritual, where there is still an interdependence that may not pertain when the soul has progressed further up the tree of life or further on its journey to rejoin its source.

Another thread in this complex story of progress toward the higher self is that the setbacks are due to failures on the part of the protagonist—to flaws that have not yet been overcome. Bata tells his wife how he can be killed. Pharaoh foolishly promises her anything without knowing what she will demand (another common theme in legends; for example, in the Pwyll and Rhiannon story, in the *Mabinogion,* Pwyll promises the stranger at the gate "anything" and the stranger demands Pwyll's bride!).

Many, many hints in the story suggest that it is not meant to be taken literally. That the woman's hair has the scent of the gods yet she is the instrument of violence against Bata (their beloved) shows that she is also the instrument by which he is to be justified or sanctified. She is planted by the gods to do what she has to do. She tests him as Jehovah tests Job.

The persea tree is associated with great sacredness in Egyptian religion. There are reliefs on the walls of temples showing Djehuti, the god of wisdom and communication and of scribes, writing the names of the pharaohs on the leaves of the eternal persea tree. Two persea trees were frequently planted on either side of the entrances to temples. I have seen the stumps of them outside the entrance to the great temple of Hatshepsut at Deir el Bahri. I find it interesting that the elder brother finds Bata's heart-soul in the form of an acacia seed and revives it with water. As Marie-Louise von Franz says in Carl Jung's book *Man and His Symbols* (p. 161), "Since . . . psychic growth cannot be brought about by a conscious effort of will power, but happens involuntarily and naturally, it is in dreams frequently symbolized by the tree, whose slow, powerful, involuntary growth fulfills a definite pattern." The acacia seed becomes the revived man and presages his existence as the persea tree, the sacred tree of life on the leaves of which all wisdom is written and the records of all history are kept. The tree symbolizes the final stage of individuation.

The grove of trees Bata goes to live in is given in some versions of the story as acacia and in at least one other as pine. Both trees are symbolically associated with immortality. J. C. Cooper lists acacia's Egyptian connotations as being solar, rebirth, immortality, initiation, innocence; Christian, immortality, a moral life; Hebrew, the Shittah tree, the sacred wood of the Tabernacle, immortality, a moral life, innocence. Of the pine's associations Cooper says this: "uprightness; straightness; vitality; fertility; strength of character; silence; solitude; phallic. As evergreen it signifies immortality." For the Egyptians it was the emblem of Serapis, the bull god, continuously reincarnated.

Either tree would therefore symbolically fit the story of the two brothers. I have chosen the acacia because it seems to fit better symbolically and physically with the landscape of Egypt as I know it. If it were in fact a pine, the land he fled to would probably be Lebanon, whose cedars are famous.

Another important thread in the story should not be missed. Bata is strong and virile. It is this that attracts his brother's wife. In some versions of the story Bata cuts off his penis and throws it into the river during his protestations to his brother that he is innocent. He is therefore a eunuch when his wife is created for him. It was his sexual attractiveness that gained him the attention of his brother's wife; it was his sexual inadequacy that lost him the attention of his own wife. He appeared later as a seed, a bull, two trees—all symbols of fertility and regeneration. Before he can be pharaoh (i.e., master of himself) he has to overcome the vagaries of fortune brought about by the sexual side of his nature. The restless and rampant bull has to become a rooted and patient tree, and the tree has to be transformed into a fully conscious man—a man who has realized his higher self.

Sources of myth
  William Kelly Simpson, ed., *The Literature of Ancient Egypt*.
  M. V. Seton-Williams, *Egyptian Legends and Stories*.

Roger Lancelyn Green, *Tales of Ancient Egypt*.
George Hart, *Egyptian Myths*.
Ineni, Papyrus No. 10183.
J. C. Cooper, *An Illustrated Encyclopaedia of Traditional Symbols*.
Carl Jung, *Man and His Symbols*.
Keith Dowman, *Masters of Enchantment*.
Moyra Caldecott, *Crystal Legends* and *Daughter of Amun*.

The Singing Tree

Arabian

The sultan of Persia sometimes walked in disguise through the city to observe his people. One night in company with his vizier he overheard the conversation of three sisters. One wished she could marry the sultan's baker so that she could eat her fill of his delicious bread. The second wished she could marry the sultan's chief cook so that she could eat her fill of the dinners he cooked. But the youngest sister wished she could marry the sultan himself and have a son.

"When he cries, his tears will be pearls. His hair on one side of his head will be silver, and on the other gold. His lips will be like rosebuds," she said.

Taking it into his head to grant their wishes, the sultan charged the vizier to bring the three young women to him on the following day.

After their initial astonishment and excitement the two elder sisters became jealous of their younger sister, who had become one of the sultan's wives and lived in great luxury. When her son was born, they took him away and placed him in a basket and set it to float down the river. They showed a dog to the sultan and told him their sister had given birth to a dog.

The chief gardener found the child in the basket, and as he and his wife had no children, he was delighted to bring him up as his own son.

When the youngest sister gave birth to a second son, the jealous sisters did the same as before. This time they declared that their sister had given birth to a cat. The sultan was very angry with his wife but gave her one more chance. The third child was a daughter, and this time the sisters showed the sultan a stick. He was beside himself with rage and locked up his wife in a shed.

Her children, meanwhile, were brought up lovingly by the chief gardener and his wife. When the time for retirement came, they moved to a beautiful house in the country. There the two princes and the princess grew up in comfortable and pleasant surroundings while their mother suffered the discomfort and indignity of imprisonment.

The gardener and his wife eventually died, and the three young people continued to live pleasantly in the house they had inherited—cheerful and content as the day was long.

One day an old woman came to the house and asked if she could pray in their little private chapel. During the conversation the princess asked her what she thought of the house and garden. The old woman replied that they were beautiful, but that they lacked three things.

Surprised, the princess questioned her further.

"The speaking bird," the old woman told her, "that draws all birds to it. The singing tree, and the golden water that, if placed in a bowl, rises like a fountain that never stops spouting and yet never overflows the bowl." She told the princess that all these wonders were to be found near India.

The princess, who had been so content until then, began to wish for those things. The old woman told her that if she wanted to find them she was to follow the road to the east for twenty days and then ask the first person she met.

When the young woman told her brothers how much she wanted those three things, the first said he would set off on the road the old woman indicated and would fetch them for her. He left his knife with his sister and told her that she must look at it every day. If he was in trouble it would become stained with blood.

After twenty days he met an old man—a wise and holy dervish—under a tree. He asked the way but could not understand the old man's reply because his hair was so long it covered his mouth. The young man cut off some of the hair and began to understand the dervish's words: a warning that the quest was extremely dangerous. The prince was not to be put off, so the dervish gave him a bowl and told him to throw it before him and follow it. The bowl would stop at the foot of a mountain.

"You must leave your horse there and continue up the mountain on foot," the dervish told him. "You will find the mountain full of black stones, and you will be confused by a cacophony of voices giving you advice, insulting you and abusing you. Take no notice, and above all, do not look behind you. If you do, you too will be turned into a black stone. At the top of the mountain you will find a bird in a cage. He will tell you where the singing tree and the golden water are."

The young man set off in good heat but soon began to be troubled by the voices that called him a fool for believing that such things as the speaking bird, the singing tree, and the golden water existed. Others threatened him with terrible dangers and made him afraid. He could not resist an anxious glance over his shoulder to see who was following him and shouting such things. As soon as he turned his head he was transformed into a black stone.

That day his sister looked at his knife and saw it stained with blood. His brother at once set off in search of him, leaving his sister with a string of pearls.

"As long as the pearls run freely through your fingers you will know that I am all right. But if they remain fixed you will know I am in trouble."

All happened to him as had happened to his brother. He too could not stop himself being distracted from his purpose by the screeching, cacophonous voices. Like his brother and so many before him, he became a black stone.

When the pearls ceased to run through her fingers the young woman herself mounted a horse and set off toward India.

After talking to the dervish she decided to stop her ears with plugs of cotton so that she would not hear the voices. Thus she managed to reach the top of the mountain and find the speaking bird. As soon as she seized hold of the cage the voices stopped. The bird told her where she would find the golden water. He also told her to go to a certain wood, break off a bough from a particular tree, and plant it in her garden. He also advised her to sprinkle the golden water on all the black stones. She did so and the spell was broken. The mountainside was full of excited and relieved people, including her two brothers.

At home she was content. The garden was full of birds that came at the call of the speaking bird, the bough took root, and the most harmonious and melodious singing came from it. The fountain of golden water sparkled and splashed, yet never dried up and never overflowed the marble bowl in which it had been placed.

One day the two brothers were out hunting when their paths crossed that of the sultan. He liked the look of the two young men so much that he invited them back to his palace. But the brothers said they would have to tell their sister before they could come. When they returned home that night they forgot to mention it to her, and the next day they had to tell the sultan that they could not come yet. This went on for several days until at last the sultan placed a small ball in the garment of the eldest. That night when he undressed the ball fell to the ground and reminded him that he had promised the sultan to tell his sister they were invited to the sultan's palace.

The sister suggested they should consult the bird. The bird advised them to accept the invitation but also, when they were at the palace, to invite the sultan back to their home for a visit.

This they did. As the young woman prepared for the sultan's visit the bird advised her to take a cucumber and stuff it with pearls—pearls that could be found in a box hidden under the tree.

When the sultan was at dinner he was astonished at the cucumber stuffed with pearls. He could not believe he was expected to eat such a vegetable, or indeed that such a vegetable existed.

The bird lost no time in pointing out that he had been prepared to believe that his wife had given birth to a dog, a cat, and a stick and yet he would not believe that a cucumber could contain pearls. It also told him the whole story of the jealous sisters.

Ashamed and contrite, the sultan released his wife, and the family were joyfully reunited.

꧁ COMMENT ꧂

Several themes in this story recur in stories throughout the world, such as the three sisters, the youngest being the most beautiful, the best, the wisest. As in the Cinderella story, the youngest suffers the jealousy of the two elder sisters. As in the Welsh story of Rhiannon, the wife is the victim of calumny. In this Arabian story her sisters get rid of her children and lie to her husband about them—and the man believes them! In the Welsh story the nurses tell the husband that the wife has torn her child apart and show him the bones and blood of an animal to prove it—and similarly he believes them. The innocent mother is punished severely and unjustly but is eventually vindicated after a long, difficult period. The gullible husband repents and is forgiven instantly.

Although the world is an unjust place and the innocent often suffer at the hands of the cruel and the jealous, and the gullible often believe what they are told (especially by the media!), these stories surely have a deeper meaning.

As is often the case, the three sisters represent the three aspects, or levels of consciousness, of one person. The first one wants to marry the baker and live on the most mundane level of physical survival. The second wants a little more out of life. But only the third seeks to fulfill her yearning to be creative. That the child is associated in her mind with pearls, with silver and gold, with rose petals indicates that she not only yearns to be creative by bringing a life into the world but wants that life to be precious, beautiful, special. She wants the love of the highest being, not of his servants (his lesser selves).

The sultan plays the role of the deity, or, as some would say, blind fate. He grants the three young women exactly what they wished for. Here is another potent theme in legends and myths. We are warned time and again to know exactly what we are asking for when we pray, for praying is not a game. It has very real consequences.

Why does the sultan not see through the lies of the two elder sisters? Perhaps he does but knows that an action has been started that must be seen through to the end. The woman has three children. When she asked to be his wife she only partially understood what that meant. Through the struggles of her children she will reach her ultimate goal: blissful union with the highest she can envisage. As she is the more spiritually aware part of the composite being that is taken into the palace, her children are the more spiritually aware part of herself—and her youngest, her daughter, the most spiritually aware of all.

That she loses them and finds them again is part of the adventure on which she has so blindly embarked. She loses part of herself, and only when that part of herself is returned to her, proved, tried, and triumphant, is she really ready to take her place at the sultan's side.

The dog, the cat, and the stick represent the worldly attitude of ordinary people to the children of the spirit. They cannot see them as they are, just as the cacophonous voices on the mountain cannot accept that there really is a talking bird, a singing tree, and golden water.

The two brothers are courageous enough to go on the quest but fail to achieve the goal. To seek spiritual awareness in the fullest sense—the talking bird (the teaching and communication of wisdom), the singing tree (the joy of wisdom), the golden water (the regenerative power of wisdom)—is difficult and dangerous. The brothers failed to obey the rules guarding the source of wisdom. They looked back in fear. They were not ready to leave what they had always known. They listened to other people's advice and warnings. Like the sultan (if we don't give him the role of deity) they listen to malicious gossip.

Note that the two boys and the girl are content and happy in their pleasant environment. The boys would probably have remained so had the girl—the embryo higher self—not begun to yearn for the three magical treasures. It is their love for her that makes them go in search of these treasures, and it is probably because the quest is not their own that they fail. But the girl wants these three symbolic gifts more than anything else in the world and seriously tries with all her faculties to attain them, even to ignoring her very natural fears.

Who is the dervish who advises them? The dervishes are a group of mystics within the Islamic tradition. I had the pleasure and privilege of seeing them once during one of their prayer-meditations when they whirled continuously and gracefully for a long time, pivoting on the center of their being and concentrating on their God. The dervish is the wise man, the religious sage, the guide to the higher self. He tells the questers what they must do. He warns and advises them. But he cannot perform the quest for them.

Why the bowl thrown ahead to show the way? Perhaps it is symbolic of the begging bowl. On this quest one must leave all considerations of worldly security and survival behind. One must take no heed for the morrow, for the lilies of the field "toil not, neither do they spin" but are clothed more magnificently than "Solomon in all his glory" (Matthew 5:28-29). It is difficult to attend to the proper progress toward spiritual enlightenment and fulfillment if one is continually distracted and overwhelmed by material considerations.

"When the bowl stops"—a moment will come when you will know that this phase of your life is over and you are ready for the next. But the empty bowl that shows the way presages the bowl that eventually contains the regenerative water that never dries up.

Why black stones? Black equals darkness—the opposite of illumination. Stone equals lifelessness. But even the black stones can be redeemed when the final illumination is achieved by the higher self.

The youngest child, the girl, the intuitive one, uses her mind as well as her courage and her intuition. She understands her limitations and takes precautions against them. She plugs her ears, knowing that she may not be able to resist succumbing to the voices. It is necessary to "know thyself" in order to succeed in this quest.

Why the bird in a cage? The girl has attained enough wisdom to listen to her own inner voice, but the voice is still within the cage of her body. It is part of herself, though it has the potential for free and soaring flight.

The harmonious and melodious voices of the singing tree are very different from the cacophonous and discordant voices on the way up the mountain.

The water that looks like flowing gold is contained in the bowl of the human heart (the bowl the three seekers followed to the foot of the mountain?). This spiritual "liquid" never dries up, never becomes stagnant. It continually replenishes itself and is always fresh. It may well renew and regenerate itself from the great invisible ocean of consciousness from which we all come and to which we all return.

When the three magical treasures are installed in her garden the time has come at last for the mother's redemption to begin. The two lower selves are still hesitant to go the whole way. They easily forget their mission and have to be reminded by the sultan with the device of the falling ball. Does the ball denote the earth? With the dropping of the earth away from their minds, they remember.

When the sultan sees that the girl has the three attributes of true wisdom he is ready to accept her mother at last, and the mother is united in splendor with her husband and her children. She has reached the transcendent state that she was blindly reaching for when she first wished to marry the sultan. All parts of her being are now enlightened and aware, and those that are not she has discarded (her sisters). She accepts her fate—both the difficulties that beset her and the rewards she ultimately receives—joyfully and without recrimination. She is complete, whole.

Source of myth
"The Three Sisters," *The Arabian Nights.*

Daphne and the Laurel Tree

Greek

Jove learned that Fate had decreed that because of man's sin "a time would come when sea and earth and the dome of the sky would blaze up, and the massive structure of the universe collapse in ruins." In an attempt to avert this he decided to wash the earth and its inhabitants away In a mighty flood. As the waters rolled through the forests dolphins "dashed against high branches, shaking the oak trees as they knocked against them." Only one man and one woman were deemed good enough to escape alive: Deucalion and his wife, Pyrrha. They managed to keep afloat and in the end their boat grounded on the top of Mount Parnassus, raised like an island above the sea.

They prayed to the gods and consulted the oracle of Themis. She advised them "to throw the bones of their great mother behind them." At first they were shocked that she should ask them to desecrate the grave of their mother, but then they began to understand that she meant their "great mother"—the earth. Deciding that she meant the hard stones were the bones of their mother earth, they walked on, throwing stones behind them. The stones softened and became men and women, a new race for the world. Other life-forms emerged from the mud and silt of the

flood. One was a fearsome and gigantic python to terrorize the newborn world.

Apollo fought against this being and finally killed it. But he made the mistake of taunting Cupid for not being as skillful as he with bow and arrow. Annoyed, Cupid shot two arrows from the top of Parnassus. One hit Apollo and one hit Daphne: the first to kindle love, the second to reject it.

Daphne wandered the woods, worshipping the huntress goddess Artemis/Diana. She was so beautiful that she was constantly pursued by men, but Cupid's arrow ensured that she rejected all suitors.

When Apollo saw her he fell instantly in love. "As the light stubble blazes up in a harvested field . . . so the god was all on fire, his whole heart . . . aflame. . . . He looked at her lips, and wanted to do more than look at them. He praised her fingers, her hands and arms, bare almost to the shoulder. Her hidden charms he imagined lovelier still."

But Daphne ran off, swifter than the wind's breath, and would not listen to his flattery.

He pursued her, calling and pleading.

Through rough places the chase went on—through fields, forests, and marshes. Apollo boasted that he was the son of Jove, the lord of Delphi, and that he had done great deeds—not least the invention of healing with herbs. "But alas," he added sadly, "there are no herbs to cure love."

But she would not listen and ran from him again, her hair streaming out behind her, her beauty "enhanced by her flight."

Then he gave up sweet words and pursued her as a hound pursues a hare. At last, exhausted and almost captured, she prayed to her father Peneus, the river god, to work a transformation and destroy the beauty that made her "quarry to men."

"Her prayer was scarcely ended when a deep languor took hold of her limbs, her soft breast was enclosed in thin bark, her hair grew into leaves, her arms into branches, and her feet that were lately so swift were held fast by sluggish roots." She had become a laurel tree.

Weeping inconsolably, Apollo embraced and kissed her trunk and branches. He swore that for evermore the laurel tree would be his emblem.

◦ COMMENT ◦

The story of Daphne and Apollo can be taken in several ways. Women might read it as the story of men's intolerable pressure on them to give up their virginity. Others might take it as the story of the life-force transforming one form into another through the energy generated by attraction and repulsion. It might make us aware that we are so much a part of the natural world that we can slip from form to form without difficulty, and we are by no means superior to nature as the Bible and its interpreters might have us believe. We could even read it as simply a warning not to cut down trees, for they are of the same nature as ourselves.

Another thread runs through the story, as it runs through other stories, other myths, and other religions and disturbs us wherever we may find it. Cupid's darts are responsible for Apollo's love and Daphne's rejection of it. Apollo and Daphne are victims, not protagonists. We are faced with the old dilemma: do we have free will or is everything we do determined? If everything we do is engineered by a force outside ourselves, how can we be accountable for our actions? How can we be praised or blamed, rewarded or punished, for the good and evil that we do? We surely cannot be held responsible if the choice has not been ours. In Ovid's *Metamorphosis* (Book LX, p. 215) even Jove admits that he cannot alter fate. There is a higher manipulator even than he.

And yet we are held responsible. We *are* responsible.

Daphne cannot help rejecting Apollo; Cupid, the higher force, has seen to that. But it is *her* decision to call on the river god to destroy her beauty and her womanhood.

The laurel that she becomes and the laurel that Apollo in his despair adopts as his sacred plant is the same laurel that contains cyanide and potassium, according to Robert Graves, and that the Pythean priestess, Apollo's oracle at Delphi, chews on to drive herself into a dangerous prophetic frenzy.

Robert Graves, in Volume I of *The Greek Myths* (p. 17), rejects the Freudian analysis of the story, which claims that Daphne represents all young girls frightened of the sex act, and points out that Daphne is a huntress, her name means "the bloody one," and her priestesses are known to hunt down travellers in remote places and tear them apart like a pack of wild dogs. It is her power and her independence she protects when she runs from him: the huntress hunted, "the bloody one" hunted by higher forces until she gives in and accepts transformation into a more peaceful form.

Whatever the explanation, the marvellous white marble statue of her at the point of transformation into a tree in the Borghese Gallery in Rome gives us feelings of fear and pursuit, of desire and frustration. It is erotic, tragic, and beautiful; once seen, it can never be forgotten.

The story of Apollo and Daphne is probably more than the story of male and female caught in forces beyond their control; I also see Apollo representing the part of us (male *or* female) that is in constant pursuit of the higher self, which constantly eludes us, transforming into something other than we expect if and when we finally catch up with it.

We are drawn to the unknown and the unobtainable, and by its very nature we can never have it.

The laurel becomes the means by which Apollo can commune with the gods at Delphi. It was not what he thought he was pursuing—but perhaps it was what he really *was* pursuing without realizing it.

The ancient Greeks had so many myths and legends about humans transforming into other forms that Ovid, the Roman poet, living from 43 B.C.E. to A.D. 17, wrote an entire work of fifteen volumes in epic verse about the phenomenon, called *Metamorphoses*. Many of the stories describe incidents in which humans are transformed (metamorphosed) into trees.

To understand why there are so many stories illustrating this theme we should perhaps remember two things about the ancient Greeks. Not only were they pre-Christian, belonging to a completely different religious tradition from Hebrews, Christians, and Muslims, but the ideas of Pythagoras regarding metempsychosis and reincarnation were familiar and acceptable to them.

Pythagoras was born on Samos but fled its tyranny to voluntary exile and finally settled at Crotona. There he began to impart some of his great knowledge and wisdom. Seeing that the fear of death was one of the major causes of our wasting our potential, he taught that "'our souls are immortal, and are received into new homes, where they live and dwell, when they have left their previous abode. I myself at the time of Trojan War—for I remember it well—'says Pythagoras, 'was Panthous' son, Euphorbus, who once received full in the breast the heavy spear of Menelaus. . . .All things change,' he said, 'but nothing dies; the spirit wanders hither and thither, taking possession of what limbs it pleases . . . but never at any time does it perish. Like pliant wax which, stamped with new designs, does not remain as it was, or keep the same shape, but yet is still itself, so I tell you that the soul is always the same but incorporates itself in different forms . . .'" (Ovid, *Metamorphoses*, Book XV, p. 339).

In Book VI of Virgil's *Aeneid*, Anchises in the world of the dead shows his son how souls hover over the river Lethe, waiting to be reborn.

Hand in hand with the belief in reincarnation goes the belief (with which no one even today would quarrel) that nothing is constant in the whole world. Everything is in a state of flux, ". . . our own bodies are ceaselessly changing, and what we have been, or now are, we shall not be tomorrow. . . . Helen weeps . . . when she sees herself in a glass, wrinkled with age, and asks herself why she was twice carried off. . . . Nor does anything retain its own appearance permanently. Even inventive nature continually produces one shape from another. Nothing in the entire universe ever perishes, believe me, but things vary, and adopt a new form. The phrase 'being born' is used for beginning to be something different from what one was before, while 'dying' means ceasing to be the same. Though this thing may pass into that, and that into this, yet the sum of things remains unchanged" (Ovid, *Metamorphoses*, Book XV, p. 341).

Given that these ideas were current in the world at the time these myths and legends were formulated, it is not surprising that Ovid could find so many stories of metamorphosis that he filled fifteen books with them.

To the Greeks all nature, animate and inanimate, was at the very least infused with the life force, but any part of it at any time could also be infused with the supernatural, the divine. This concept is not so foreign to us. We can still see "heaven in a grain of sand" in our better moments, as William Blake said. In the Gnostic "Gospel of Thomas," 95:26-28, we read, "Cleave a piece of wood, I am there; lift up the stone and you will find me there." But for many centuries we have rejected the ancient classical form of pantheism.

Our reason, our science, our intellectual questing have led us far away from the sense of the holiness and wholeness of nature infused with divinity, towards a bitter and sterile world where we are allowed to exploit and spoil everything in the name of "progress." Progress toward what? In a world where our trees are dying from acid rain, our forests are giving way to deserts, and every day a precious irreplaceable species of animal or plant becomes extinct, we must surely wonder whether we were not too quick to dismiss the ancient wisdom, expressed as it might have been too quaintly for our sophisticated palates. If only we had considered before it was too late the truths contained in these ancient myths and legends. As Theodolphus, Bishop of Orleans at the time of Charlemagne, said, ". . . many a truth is to be found hidden beneath a covering of fiction" (quoted by Mary M. Innes on p. 19 of her introduction of Ovid's *Metamorphoses*).

Because everything was infused with the same life force and nothing was ever destroyed or lost but rather changed and transformed, it did not seem at all odd that a man or woman could literally change into a tree. Today we know that the tree and the human body are made up of the same waves and particles, each vibrating at a different rate. It is not inconceivable, therefore, that if the rate of vibration were changed the form could also be changed. The Greek gods represent certain aspects of the natural world, named and personified purely for convenience to make the mystery at the root of existence seem less mysterious and to enable us to go about our business less distracted by unanswerable questions. That there are so many legends about gods making love to humans is not an accident. If we say that all the different realms interact and are interdependent, from cases in which the rate of the vibration of matter is at such a high frequency that almost invisible, intangible forms have been brought about (for example, gods, nymphs, etc.) to the cases in which the lower frequency of the vibration has brought about the grosser forms of matter, we find that the "gross" often reach up, dreaming of becoming "less gross," while the "less gross" often long for the sensations of the "gross" denied to them in their ethereal form. To put it another way, everything that exists is dependent on the balance of action and reaction, the urge to merge and the urge to break away. Attraction and repulsion drives the motor from the subatomic level through the human "war of the sexes" to the mighty spirit dramas where good and evil perpetually battle.

Sources of myth

Ovid, *Metamorphoses*, Book I.
Robert Graves, *The Greek Myths*.

The Myrrh Tree

Greek

King Cynyras of Cyprus was the grandson of Pygmalion and the ivory statue to which Venus had granted life. He had a daughter, Princess Myrrha. Suitors came from far and wide to woo her, but she would have none of them. She was in love with her father, and no matter how she fought against this love she could not conquer it. She told herself that no law of nature forbade such a love, as animals frequently mated within their families and some nations likewise condoned it. But guilt consumed her, and at last she decided to take her own life rather than live one more sleepless and agonizing night.

Her nurse, sleeping at her door, heard a sound and came into the chamber to find Myrrha trying to hang herself. She took her in her arms, tried to comfort her, and pleaded with her to tell her what the trouble was. But the princess would only weep and turn her face away. Only when the nurse threatened to tell the king, her father, that she had tried to kill herself did Myrrha's reactions give the nurse a hint of the girl's guilty secret. Shocked, the nurse drew back, but as she could see that Myrrha was determined to die if she could not have her father as lover, she decided to take matters into her own hands.

During the festival of Ceres, when all married women were away from their husband's beds performing the rites of the corn goddess, the nurse persuaded the king to take a young unmarried girl to bed with him. Dazed with wine, he readily agreed, and Myrrha was led to him in darkness. Three times she stumbled. Three times an owl screeched a warning. But, afraid though she was, she could not stop herself.

That night she lay with him and conceived a child.

The next night and the next the same scene was enacted—the secret lovemaking under cover of darkness. At last the king, curious to see what his mistress looked like, lit a lamp and looked into his daughter's face.

Horrified, he seized his sword, but she slipped away into the night.

Myrrha wandered homeless and afraid for nine months. Then, unable to go on any longer, she pleaded with the gods to help her. She asked to be changed into some other form altogether, as she had disgraced the form of woman. "If I live, I pollute the lives of those around me. If I die, I will pollute the dead."

"Earth heaped itself round her legs as she spoke and roots, breaking out through her toe-nails, stretched sideways, forming foundations for a tall trunk. Her bones were changed into hard wood and through the marrow, which survived in their interior, flowed sap instead of blood. Her arms became large branches, her fingers smaller ones, and her skin hardened into bark" (Ovid, *Metamorphoses,* Book X, p. 238).

When the time came for the birth of her child she could no longer cry out, for she was a tree. But so mournfully did the swollen tree bend over, and so many were the drops of resin that fell from its bark like sweat or tears, that nymphs took pity on her and prayed for the child's release. At once the bark split open and a beautiful baby boy fell out of the tree. The nymphs took him up in their arms and cared for him until he became a handsome man. They named him Adonis, and he became the beloved of Venus herself.

The myrrh tree, however, has ever since been associated with penance, sorrow, and suffering.

ॡ COMMENT ॡ

Myrrh is exuded as resin from a tree and was an important ingredient of the oil used for anointing kings (Exodus 30:23–33). It was presented to the infant Jesus by one of the three magi and was offered to him on the cross to ease his pain. Afterward it was used in the tomb with aloes and other spices.

The story of Myrrha reminds us that myrrh was used in ancient days in female purification rites. The princess cannot control her sexual desires, and to the Greeks, who believed in moderation in all things, this represented not only a danger to the balance of nature but also a danger to the social order. Other countries, notably Egypt, had no taboo against incest, but Greece had, and any action that put the social order in jeopardy was condemned. This is a sad story of a conflict within a woman between her natural instincts and the dictates of social order. It is an all-too-common drama. She as woman is destroyed by it, but she survives as a tree, as nothing is ever truly destroyed. Her son is beloved of the gods, for he is innocent of any wrongdoing—the Greeks had no law that required children to pay for the sins of their parents. We are heartened to see that no matter how tarnished the relationship of the parents may be, new life—innocent and pure—can come forth from it and be accepted with no reservations.

Sources of myth
   Ovid, *Metamorphoses*, Book X.
   Joseph Campbell, *The Mythic Image*, Vol. III.

Persephone
and the
Pomegranate Tree

Greek

Persephone, the daughter of Demeter, a great earth goddess, was picking flowers in a meadow beneath the slopes of Mount Etna in Sicily one sunny day, when suddenly a gigantic shadow crossed the sun, the earth rumbled and shook, and the air became hot and sulphurous. She looked up in alarm, her hand around the stem of a narcissus flower. Above her towered an iron chariot. It was drawn by four black horses, nostrils flaring, eyeballs glaring, flanks steaming. Holding the reins and staring directly into her eyes stood a tall figure. His black cloak flowed out like smoke-shadow over the landscape, and where it touched the earth the grass withered and the flowers died. It seemed to Persephone she heard her companions shrieking in the distance like so many startled birds, but close around her there was a terrible silence. She had never seen a man so tall and strong, so dark-eyed, so storm-browed. With one hand he held the reins; with the other he reached out to her. She cringed back but could not run. She tried to scream but found that no sound came from her throat. The man stepped down. He approached her. Over the child of

Demeter and Zeus the dark king's shadow fell, and as she looked up at him she could no longer see the blue sky, no longer see the sun's golden rays, no longer see the trees, the meadows, and the silver shimmering sea. She could see only one thing.

She dropped the flowers she held.

She turned to run, but now it was too late. The dark king had her by the arm and drew her to him roughly.

Her companions saw her dragged into the chariot and driven off. Black, sulphurous fumes billowed across the landscape and hid the direction they were taking. Screaming, the maidens rushed to the throne of Zeus and pleaded to be turned into birds to follow the chariot and see where it was going. In their impatience to be going they left the throne of Zeus winged and clawed, but still breasted like women. As sirens they pursued the chariot, and as sirens they remained forevermore. They could not follow Hades, the dark king, to the dark regions of the underworld, but they haunted the regions above, bitter and frustrated, luring sailors to their deaths and interfering in the affairs of men.

Past Cerberus, the many-headed dog that guarded the entrance to the underworld, Persephone was taken. Over the dark river she was ferried by Charon, the ferryman. There in the gloomy palace of the king of the dead she was released at last from Hades' iron grip. To every direction she ran, but there was no way out. Weeping, she pleaded to be returned to the bright and flowering fields, to the warmth of her mother, to the companionship of her friends. Hades would not listen. He led her into a banqueting hall and set before her a feast fit for a queen. He placed a rich jeweled crown upon her head and strung jewels around her neck and her arms. With a stern yet passionate speech he offered her his kingdom and all that he possessed.

Trembling, she refused everything. Pale and hungry, she would not eat. She tore the crown from her head and flung it to the floor.

Time passed and yet did not pass. Persephone ran from chamber to chamber in the terrible palace and at last found her way to the garden. There black poplars stood around, no breeze stirring their shadowy leaves. Barren willows hung limply over black water. The only flowers she could see were asphodel—the flowers of the grave.

"Oh, Lady," cried Hades, ever pursuing her. "I will not let you go. See, here is a tree—a pomegranate tree. You are hungry. Eat."

In the midst of the black and blighted garden stood a green pomegranate tree laden with ripe and glowing fruit. The distraught girl flung her arms around its trunk, her tears watering its roots. She was hungry. Here was fruit. She picked. She ate. She sank to the ground and rested herself. She fell asleep.

When she woke she was in a spacious bed with the lord of the underworld beside her. Her head was nestling on his arm. His leg was intertwined with hers.

Was he really so dark and fierce? Was he not handsome? Her body stirred to his and they made love.

In the world above, Demeter was in despair at the loss of her daughter. She searched the world for a sign of her. No one knew where she had gone until Hermes, who as messenger of the gods passed from time to time into the underworld and out again, reported seeing her on the throne beside Hades, wearing a jeweled crown, her small white hand clinging affectionately to the arm of the lord of death.

Demeter was so angry she stormed about the earth and the earth knew no respite from her anger. Gales snapped the trees and blew houses away. Ice closed the lakes and ponds. Rivers dried up. All nature suffered and mourned with the great earth goddess.

Zeus, hearing the complaints of his people, called her to this throne. Angrily she told her story and added, "Persephone is your daughter, albeit conceived in rape. Why have you done nothing to recover her?"

She ranted on and on while the green and living earth turned to dust.

Zeus at last put up his hand. There was little that he, great god though he was, could do against Hades, his own brother. The two were equally matched—the one who lived in light and the one who lived in dark, lord of life and lord of death. Each was king of his own realm.

"If she has eaten nothing in the kingdom of Hades," he said at last, "there is a chance we can recover her."

But Persephone had eaten the fruit of the pomegranate tree, and Zeus could do nothing to give her back to her mother.

"She has chosen marriage. She has chosen her husband. I cannot . . ."

"Cannot!" shrieked Demeter. "Cannot!" Her scorn was so great, and her hold on him so strong from the lust he once had had for her and the rape he had perpetrated on her, that he sent Hermes down to negotiate with his brother, the king of death.

At last it was agreed that for half the year Persephone would dwell above in the light with her mother, the earth burgeoning with bud and flower and fruit. The other half of the year she would dwell with her husband in the underworld, and the earth would lie dormant in cold and dark, waiting for her return—her mother clad in mourning, biding her time until her daughter rejoined her in the spring.

COMMENT

As we know, myths and legends never do just one thing, and that is their strength. The Persephone myth grew up to explain natural phenomena; that is clear. But did it not also explore the psyche as well—Hades representing not only death but the dark side of ourselves? Persephone voluntarily, though under persuasion, ate the pomegranate fruit that precluded her from going back to the pure life of the maiden. The pomegranate in Greek myth is the fruit of commitment to marriage and sexual maturity. She could have refused to eat, as could Eve in Eden, but like Eve she did not. Having eaten, she found her perception changed. Hades no longer seemed repulsive. Her sexuality was aroused and she loved him—but perhaps never fully. She did not protest about going back to her mother's realm for half the year. Like us she is half light and half dark, and the tension between the two is a powerful driving force in life. The balance of alternating rest periods and growing periods in nature is healthy and necessary, as it is in ourselves.

The Greeks are not alone in producing this myth to explain the contrast between winter and summer and the conflict of dark and light in our souls. Iduna, the Norse goddess of spring who gave the gods the apples of youth, has to spend some time each year in the storm-giant's dark mansion.

Manly P. Hall, in *The Secret Teachings of All Ages* (pp. xcv and xcvi), goes into the symbolism of the pomegranate. He says that the pomegranate in the story of Persephone signifies the sensuous life which, once tasted, temporarily deprives man of immortality. Also on account of its vast number of seeds the pomegranate was often employed to represent natural fecundity. For the same reason, Jacob Bryant in his *Analysis of Ancient Mythology* (1774) notes that the ancients recognized in this fruit an appropriate emblem of the Ark of the Deluge, which contained the seeds of the new human race. Among the Ancient Mysteries the pomegranate was also considered to be a divine symbol of such peculiar significance that its true explanation could not be divulged. It was termed by the Cabiri "the forbidden secret." Many Greek gods and goddesses are depicted holding the fruit or flower of the pomegranate in their hands, evidently to signify that they are givers of life and plenty. Pomegranate capitals were placed upon the pillars of Joachin and Boaz standing in front of King Solomon's Temple; and by the order of Jehovah, pomegranate blossoms were embroidered upon the bottom of the High Priest's ephod.

Persephone accepts the many sides of life held together in one whole when she accepts the upper and the lower worlds.

Meinrad Craighead, in her book *The Sign of the Tree*, writes that the pomegranate came to represent for the early Christians the unity of the Church: "many seeds held together in one rounded fruit."

Sources of myth

A. R. Hope Moncrieff, *Classic Myth and Legend*.
Larousse Encyclopaedia of Mythology.
Jean Lang, *Book of Myths*.
Meinrad Craighead, *The Sign of the Tree: Meditations in Images and Words*.
Manly P. Hall, *The Secret Teachings of All Ages*.

Orpheus

S oon after the wedding, Eurydice, the bride of the poet Orpheus, was bitten by a snake and died.

Filled with sorrow, Orpheus followed her to the underworld. There, singing and playing his lyre, he pleaded with Persephone and her dark lord for her release.

"If you do not grant her a reprieve," he said, "keep me too, for I cannot live without her."

All in the underworld were moved to tears by the beauty and pathos of his song, and he was granted the life of Eurydice on one condition—that he not look back until he was clear of the regions of death.

Orpheus and Eurydice struggled up the steep path toward the world of the living. They had nearly reached it when Orpheus glanced back to make sure Eurydice was still close behind him. Instantly she was gone into the dark mists. He had lost her.

Weeping, he tried to rush after her, but the ferryman refused to let him cross the Styx a second time. Bitterly he mourned her and his own foolishness, but the gods of the underworld refused to listen.

Orpheus lived on. His handsome face and beautiful songs attracted many women, but he would have nothing to do with them. Young boys sometimes pleased him, but no woman.

All nature loved his music. At times he sat on the top of a bare hill, and before he had finished his song the trees from the valleys had gathered round him and he was enclosed in a leafy glade rich in oak, hazel, laurel, ash, fir, sycamore, and maple. Even willows left the riverbank to gather round and hear his songs. His most constant companion was the cypress, who itself had once been a boy who pleaded to mourn forever for the beautiful stag he had inadvertently slain, and was now the friend of all who mourned the loss of a loved one.

Animals and birds gathered, all listening to the poems and songs of Orpheus.

Certain wild Ciconian women, devotees of the Dionysian cult, seeing this and furious that Orpheus spoke to trees and beasts and birds but scorned women, threw spears and rocks at him. At first even the weapons they threw were charmed by his singing and fell at his feet without harming him. Only when the women managed to raise such a cacophony of noise that his music could not be heard did the stones finally find their mark. They slew all around him and beat him with anything they could find until at last those lips that had softened even the hearts of the dread shades of the underworld were silent.

All nature wept for Orpheus, but he, in death at last, found his Eurydice.

On the earth above, Dionysius punished the women who had destroyed the gentle Orpheus by turning them into gnarled old oak trees.

"Just as a bird, finding its legs caught in the hidden snare of some cunning fowler, beats its wings when it feels itself held, and tightens the bonds by frightened fluttering, so each of the women, as she became rooted to the spot, went mad with fear, and vainly tried to flee, while the tough root held her fast, preventing her attempts to pull herself away."

COMMENT

Here is another story in which man forfeits everything by not being able to control himself. The love and persistence of Orpheus almost rescue Eurydice from death, but he looks back, knowing that that is exactly what he must not do. Self-control within the framework of the cosmic order was one of the supreme achievements admired by the ancient Greeks. Loss of it brings about all kinds of disasters.

Like Phaeton's sisters (see next story), Orpheus cannot recover from his loss and mourns Eurydice endlessly. This is his undoing, and the jealous Ciconian women bring about his death.

That Orpheus and his lyre should charm all nature does not seem so extraordinary to us today, for we have learned that plants and animals respond to sound and to gentle, harmonious music, and that certain kindly tones of voice can have a beneficial effect on their growth and well-being.

Source of myth

Ovid, *Metamorphoses*, Books X and XI.

Phaeton's Sisters

Greek

Phaeton was the son of the Sun and of Clymene, but one day, as he was boasting about his father, a friend taunted him that he was not divinely conceived at all but that his mother had invented that story to cover her shame. Anxiously, the boy confronted his mother and demanded proof. She swore that his father was indeed the Sun and suggested that he go and ask his father himself for proof.

So Phaeton set off for the east to seek his father's palace. At length he found it. Light blazed from golden walls and columns, flickering on the ivory roof and silver doors. Exquisite images of the gods, the heavens, the earth, and the sea were engraved everywhere. The Sun was seated on his golden throne, bright with shining emeralds, and around him were grouped the hours, the days, the months, the years, the seasons, and the generations.

Trembling at the majesty of it all, the boy yet managed to say what he had come to say.

The great being at once told Phaeton that he was indeed his son. To prove it, he swore that he would grant whatever the boy wished.

Phaeton asked to ride his father's chariot for one whole day.

Horrified at the request, the Sun tried to persuade him that this was the one thing he should not ask for, because no one but himself, not even Jove, could control the horses and drive that chariot. It would be certain death for anyone else.

"If you want the proof that I am your father," he said, "see how worried I am that you should come to harm. Surely that is enough proof?"

But the young Phaeton would not listen. The god was bound by his vow; only the boy could release him—and he would not.

After trying every persuasion and warning, the Sun had to let the boy into the chariot, and Phaeton proudly took his place. But his delight was short-lived. The spirited horses ran wild when they felt unskilled and unfamiliar hands on the reins, and the whole order of nature was disturbed as the sun's chariot ran amok, scorching the earth until the rivers dried up and the earth cracked. All nature called to Jove for help, and at last he succeeded in launching his thunderbolts against the lad.

Phaeton fell flaming to his death.

Month after month his mother and his sisters stood beside his grave and mourned for him. They were inconsolable.

One day when Paethusa tried to fling herself upon the ground, she complained that she could not move her feet. "Lampetie would have gone to her assistance, but she was held fast by roots which had suddenly formed. A third made to tear her hair, and plucked out leaves. One cried out that her legs were caught in the grip of a tree trunk, another was indignant to find her arms had become long branches. While they were marvelling at this, bark surrounded their thighs, and gradually spread over womb and breast, shoulders and hands, till only their lips remained, vainly calling for their mother."

Clymene rushed from one to the other trying to pull them free, but the twigs bled when she broke them, and Phaeton's sisters screamed in agony. At last there was no sign of women's flesh. The grove of trees had increased in size by the number of Phaeton's sisters.

From the bark of some of the trees "there flowed tears which, hardened into amber by the sun, dropped from the new-made branches and were received by the shining river. It bore them off

in its waters, to be an ornament one day for Roman brides"
(Ovid, *Metamorphoses*).

COMMENT

The story of Phaeton presents a mortal trying to play the role of
a god. By doing so he risks the well-being of the whole world.

We ourselves have brought our planet almost to its end by
playing a thoughtless game with the power of nuclear fission. And
will we, like Phaeton's sisters, spend the rest of our lives in hopeless despair and mourning? Or will we keep trying to find ways
to save our planet before it really is too late?

Source of myth
Ovid, *Metamorphoses*, Books I and II.

The Golden Apples of the Hesperides

Greek

Zeus took the form of Amphitryon, grandson of Perseus, and planted the seed of Heracles (Hercules) in the womb of Alcmene, Amphitryon's wife. On the day Alcmene was due to be delivered, Zeus swore an irrevocable oath that the descendant of Perseus born that day would one day rule Greece.

Hera, the wife of Zeus, jealous of Alcmene, descended to earth and arranged that another descendant of Perseus should be brought prematurely to birth, while Alcmene's labor would be prolonged. The boy Eurystheus was therefore the inheritor of Greece, while Heracles, the son of Alcmene, was bound to him as subject.

Heracles grew strong and brave as Zeus intended, but Hera did everything in her power to destroy him. From cradle to grave he was never free of dangers and difficulties; probably he survived as long as he did only because he was befriended by another goddess, Athene.

Frustrated that every physical challenge was met and overcome by Heracles, Hera caused his mind to be attacked, and in a fit of madness he massacred his own wife and children.

In an agony of despair and regret, Heracles consulted the oracle of Delphi and was told to work out his penance under the orders of Eurystheus.

For twelve years Eurystheus, inspired by Hera, set Heracles impossible tasks, each one designed to bring about his disgrace and his death. But Heracles fought and defeated the Nemean lion, the Lernaean hydra, the wild boar of Erythmanthus, the Stymphalian birds that fed on human flesh. He captured the elusive Ceryneian hind and cleaned out in one day the stables of King Augeas, which were heaped with many years' accumulation of filth. He captured the mad bull of Minos in Crete and the man-eating mares of Diomedes. He wrestled with Death himself for the life of Alcestis and defeated the formidable warrior queen of the Amazons for her jeweled girdle. He rounded up the cattle of the monster Geryon so that Eurystheus might sacrifice them to Hera.

And then, not content with these remarkable achievements, Eurystheus demanded that Heracles bring him three golden apples from the garden of the Hesperides.

At the marriage of Zeus and Hera, the mighty earth goddess, Gaia, had given them a gift of a tree that bore golden apples. This tree was so precious to Hera that she planted it in the fabulous garden that grew beyond the gates of the world, in the land where the sun goes every night when it leaves Attica. In this mysterious realm beyond the reach of ordinary mortals, the tree was cherished and guarded by the three beautiful daughters of Atlas and Hesperus, the Hesperides.

The location of the garden was secret. Heracles was faced with a different challenge this time, for brute strength and courage alone would not serve him.

He set off with no idea where to find the garden and spent a long time wandering, encountering and defeating giants and monsters, but finding himself no nearer to the object of his quest. One day, sitting beside the estuary of the river Eridanus and musing on his lack of success, he became aware that the silver shapes flowing and floating, swirling and curling deep within the water were not fishes but water nymphs, Nereides, young women with shimmering limbs and with long streamers of hair woven with water weed and flowers.

They gathered around his reflection, laughing to see how it fragmented as they swam in and out of it. It seemed to him that his own flesh responded to their cool bodies by tingling, stirring, and rousing, though it was only his reflection they touched.

After play had exhausted the nymphs they spoke with him, and he told them what he was seeking. They themselves did not know the location of the garden of Hesperides, but they were sure their father, Nereus, would certainly know where it lay. Nereus was the ancient, wise, prophetic god of the sea, the son of Gaia, who had given the magical tree to Hera and Zeus in the first place, and he knew all there was to know.

Some nymphs who had enjoyed the encounter with the handsome hero more than the others, led him to the great sea-cave where Nereus dwelt, while the others tried to prevent his finding it.

At last Heracles stood before the ancient god and asked for the information he needed, but was refused. Nereus knew all things but was wary of giving out his knowledge to anyone lest it be misused or misunderstood.

Heracles became impatient. He seized the old man and shook him, demanding an answer to his question. But the old man slipped from his grasp like an eel and slid away. Heracles was about to catch the eel when the eel became a fish. He was about to catch the fish when it became a dolphin and leaped for the air. He was about to catch the dolphin when it became a bird. Heracles flung nets of seaweed woven by the Nereids until the creature was bound and helpless. Exhausted from the effort of such rapid and radical transformations, Nereus gave in and told him what he wanted to know.

Then Heracles set off on a long and eventful journey to the secret garden where the golden apples grew.

In Libya he was challenged to a wrestling match by Antaeus, a monstrous giant who preyed on all travellers. Antaeus was a son of Gaia, the earth, and could not be defeated as long as some part of him was in contact with his mother. After a supreme effort Heracles managed to heave him up above his head, where he was no longer in touch with the earth. There he destroyed him.

One night when he was asleep he was attacked by thousands of pygmies and could scarcely free himself from their barbs and shafts. But at last, heaving and rolling, he managed to trap them in his lionskin cloak and whirl them away from him.

In Egypt he was captured by Busiris, the king, who was wont to sacrifice a foreigner each year in an attempt to avert famine from the land. Tightly bound, Heracles yet managed to burst his bonds and escape.

In Ethiopia he battled with a fearsome king, defeating him, and placed a worthier man on the throne before he left.

He crossed the sea in a golden boat given him by the sun and came to the mountain range of the Caucasus. There he found Prometheus chained to a rock, each day an eagle gnawing his liver away, each night the liver growing again. Prometheus was suffering this punishment for having stolen fire from the gods for the use of mankind. Heracles succeeded in shooting the eagle and freeing Prometheus, who in gratitude gave him further instructions on how to reach the famous garden.

At last Heracles arrived in the far, far west, where the great sun flooded the world with such brilliant crimson and gold he feared he would be blinded. As his eyes became accustomed to the blaze of glory he could see that an island rose from the ocean—an island more beautiful than any he could have imagined. On this island were flowers that never died and trees that never withered. In the center was the tree he had come so far to seek, and dancing in the meadow around it were the beautiful daughters of Hesperus.

They laughed when he asked for some apples to take to his master Eurystheus and said that the apples were not in their power to give, for Hera had put a guardian on them that even they could not defeat.

He looked at the tree and saw that around its trunk was coiled a monstrous and deadly snake.

Then began a battle more fearsome than all the rest, Heracles struggling against the vast and muscular coils of the giant serpent and fighting to avoid its poisonous fangs. At last this monster too lay dead at his feet.

He snatched the golden apples and made all speed back to Eurystheus, believing that at last he had fulfilled his penance and would be free.

Eurystheus looked at the apples in his hand. It pained him that the hero had once again managed to avoid death and carry out his appointed task.

"Keep them," he said bitterly. "Bring me Cerberus, the guardian of the underworld, and your twelve labors will be complete."

Heracles laid the golden apples at the feet of Athene, who had championed him on several occasions against Hera's spite. This last and deadly quest could not be faced alone.

COMMENT

This particular labor of Heracles is subtly different from the others he has been asked to perform, and I think it is no accident that it comes near the end of his long and arduous initiation, or testing period.

Originally he was an athlete and performed magnificent feats of physical prowess. But as a hero destined for true greatness, more is expected of him. Hera, in this instance playing the role of the dark force, attacks his mind. He succumbs and commits a terrible crime, the guilt of which he must expiate. Year by year, through tremendous effort and dedication to duty, he defeats the dark monsters that beset the human psyche.

At last he is ready for the quest of the golden apples, the moment when all darkness is left behind and in a blaze of enlightenment he reaches up to the ultimate goal of all questing souls—the nourishment that grows in heaven alone. It is significant that Eurystheus does not accept the apples. He must know that they can be held only by the one who has sought them out and won against all odds to achieve them. It is also significant that Heracles does not keep them but presents them to his goddess. Athene then returns them to the garden, for there—and there only—they must be. It is not their possession that is important for the hero, but the quest to achieve them. It is an indication of the nobility of his now-awakened soul that he knows he must present them back to the gods. Enlightenment is no good if it is not used in the service of the deity.

But the apples cannot be won by brute strength and courage alone. Heracles must first think, plan, inquire, search. He has to do good deeds. For instance, he rescues Prometheus, and in Ethiopia he replaces a bad king by a better one. He has to break bonds that make him the victim of an old religion that demands blood sacrifice. His defeat of the son of Gaia by lifting him off the earth suggests that he cannot win the battle with himself if he does not leave earthly values behind. He travels in a boat given him by the sun—the solar boat of Ra—that sails into the otherworld when the ordinary body is left behind.

In outwitting Nereus he learns that he must not be misled by illusion. The ocean is the ocean of knowledge and wisdom, and Nereus guards it from those who are not ready for such knowledge. Heracles does not kill him but traps him in a net made from the material of his own medium, and we understand by this that a quest of the spirit must be conducted in the spirit. Heracles proves that he is not deceived by illusory transformations, and he is therefore ready for the knowledge Nereus was at first not prepared to give.

Even then, Nereus does not give him complete instructions. Heracles needs further direction from Prometheus, who also endured the punishment of the gods for something he did. His crime was not a blind, insane whim like that of Heracles but a deliberate desire to help mankind, in the course of which he offended the gods. I sometimes wonder whether the "fire" Prometheus stole from the sun was the terrible secret of nuclear fission and the gods knew what destruction this would bring to an immature mankind.

At any rate, both heroes have the painful privilege of being tested.

In several versions of this story, the sequence of the adventures Heracles has on the way to the island of the Hesperides is varied. We are led to believe that the island exists in the far western ocean beyond Gibraltar, beyond the known world at that time, yet the progress of Heracles is not direct. I believe this is important. Enlightenment is not always achieved by the direct approach; it is more likely to come upon us from the direction least expected. And in preparation there are many different things we must learn from different directions before we dare approach the garden itself. The garden is on the island—separated by its great ocean from the mundane world.

No symbol in myth worth its salt can be given an easy explanation, but I think we can safely assume that the garden of the Hesperides represents that mythical land, that garden of Eden, that new Jerusalem, that shining, timeless realm in which mortals believe they will find their higher selves.

Perhaps the garden represents the island where Enoch and Elijah are believed to wait in a state of blessedness until the final day—an island reputed to have been found and explored and claimed for Christ against the ancient pagan gods by the sixth-century Irish saint Brendan. It is on this island Heracles defeats the dark side of himself and the dark forces set against him and achieves the golden apples, the nourishment of heaven.

It is not surprising the apple tree has such significance in myth and legend. It is beautiful with blossom in spring, like a young bride entering into her most fertile and reproductive phase. Its fruit is delicious and sustaining. Colin and Liz Murray, in their book *The Celtic Tree Oracle*, say this:

> The apple card represents a choice of beauty, the beauty of life and youthfulness. Linked to this is Avalon, or the magical "Apple-land." Glastonbury is set within the Celtic Apple-lands. From the Welsh poem "Avellenau" we learn that the Bard Merlin secretly revealed to his lord the existence of this orchard. It was borne from place to place by the enchanter on all his journeyings. The ignorant, however, must not eat of its fruit, for within the Apple is contained a pythagorean pentagram. Cut it width-ways and its secrets are revealed in the shape of its pips. This gave beauty in the judgment of Paris, to Aphrodite.

J. C. Cooper, in *An Illustrated Encyclopaedia of Traditional Symbols*, says, "As the apples of the Hesperides and the fruit of Freya's garden, it symbolizes immortality. Offering an apple is a declaration of love." In Celtic mythology it has "magic and chthonic powers." It is "the fruit of the otherworld"; of fertility and of marriage. "Halloween, an apple festival, is associated with the death of the old year" and the birth of the new.

Cormac mac Airt, the Irish "Solomon," living in the third century when Tara of the kings was at its height, possessed a silver branch containing three golden apples that had been a gift from Manannan mac Lir, the god of the sea. When he shook it the sick, the wounded, and women in childbed were given rest.

The fruit eaten by Eve was associated with evil and later supposed to be an apple. Was it given this dark connotation just because the apple was such a potent symbol of pagan times?

Sources of myth

Larousse Encyclopaedia of Mythology.
A. R. Hope Moncrieff, *Classic Myth and Legend.*
Alexander S. Murray, *Manual of Mythology.*
Colin and Liz Murray, *The Celtic Tree Oracle.*
J. C. Cooper, *An Illustrated Encyclopaedia of Traditional Symbols.*

The Transformation of Dryope

Greek

Although Apollo had raped Dryope and left her with child, Andraemon took her in as wife. They lived together by a lake surrounded by myrtle groves.

One day Dryope took her son, Amphissos, to the lake edge to offer garlands to the nymphs. There she saw the purple lotus flowering and picked one for her son.

But the flower stem bled, and she dropped it in alarm. The plant had once been the nymph Lotis, fleeing the obscenities of Priapus.

Dryope, horrified at what she had done, tried to flee, but now, rooted to the ground, found herself unable to move. Her sister, who had witnessed the whole episode, ran to fetch her husband and her father.

With her last words Dryope cried out against the injustice of what was happening to her. "I am being punished without having committed any crime," she said. She charged her family to bring the child up well and allow him to play under her branches. "Let him beware of pools," she said, "and not pick flowers from trees, but believe that all fruitful shrubs are the bodies of the goddesses." When her lips stopped speaking, they ceased to be, but long after her body was transformed, the new-made branches kept their warmth.

COMMENT

This is the most disturbing of these stories, for apparently Dryope is punished without having committed any crime. If so, how can this be in a just and orderly universe? But judgment and punishment may well be human concepts irrelevant to a universe that runs on different principles entirely—among which the implacable logic of cause and effect cannot be ignored.

Source of myth
Ovid, *Metamorphoses*, Book IX.

Aeneas and the Golden Bough

Greek

Aeneas asked the Cumean sibyl if he could visit his father in the world of the dead. She replied that he could visit only if he could find the golden bough of Juno, hidden deep in a dark forest. Once finding it, he must pluck it, for Persephone, queen of the underworld, had decreed that no one might enter the hidden world of her domain without first presenting this bough. The sibyl warned him that no one could tear the bough from the tree unless the Fates had called him to the task. If it was not his destiny to pluck the bough, not even the strongest blade would prevail.

Aeneas, the son of Aphrodite and the Dardanian king, a great hero of the Trojan war, prayed to his mother that the golden bough would reveal itself to him. No sooner had he finished his prayer than two white doves flew down and landed near him. As white doves had always been associated with Aphrodite, he took this as a sign, and when they moved on he followed them. They led him to a gigantic holm-oak deep in the darkest and most inaccessible part of the forest. There, peering up through the leafy branches, he caught sight of the gleam of gold. Reaching up, Aeneas took hold of the shining bough and pulled. It broke off easily, and the stump that was left almost instantly started to re-

new itself. Triumphantly Aeneas bore the golden bough to the Cumaen sibyl.

There, beside a black lake in the gloomy forest, she prepared to sacrifice to Hecate, the hidden one, the goddess of the night. All night the two performed rituals to the gods of the underworld. Just before the dawn the earth heaved, the mountains moved, and a vast and dreadful cavern opened at their feet. Calling on Aeneas to follow her, the sibyl strode into the opening.

"They were walking in the darkness, with the shadows round them and the night's loneliness above them, through Pluto's substanceless Empire" (Virgil, *The Aeneid*, Book VI, lines 255–287).

At the center of this dark and terrifying place grew a giant elm tree, each leaf a false dream. Weird and frightening shapes surrounded them, and Aeneas drew his sword. But he soon realized that "they were bodiless, airy, lives flitting behind an empty figment of a form" (Virgil, *The Aeneid*, Book VI, lines 288–322).

The ferryman of the Styx challenged them to go back but allowed them into the boat when they showed him that they had the golden bough. "He looked in awe at the holy offering, the Wand of Destiny, which it was long since he had seen" (Virgil, *The Aeneid*, Book VI, lines 388–420).

Thus came the living Aeneas and the aged sibyl to the dreadful realm of the dead.

They passed many ghastly shapes and shades and saw many whom Aeneas had known alive. He tried to speak to them and longed to linger with them, but the sibyl hurried him away. They passed the battlements of Tartarus, where they shuddered to hear the groans and screams of those suffering the torments of punishment for their deeds on earth. At last they came to the great door of Elysium, where Aeneas "sprinkled himself with fresh water, and set the branch upright on the threshold before him." Here were found the fortunate woods and the homes of the blest and the land of joy. Here everywhere there were bright and happy spirits, soft grass, and scented bay trees.

The sibyl inquired of everyone they met where Anchises, the father of Aeneas, might be. They were guided through meadows and shady woods and glittering lands until at last they found him.

Anchises was overjoyed to see his son and reached out his hands to him, but Aeneas, trying to embrace him, found that his father was a wraith and his arms could not close on him. Three times he tried. Three times he failed.

Eagerly they conversed, Aeneas asking question after question.

He spotted the river Lethe, the river of forgetfulness, beside a wood, and "about the river, like bees in a meadow on a fine summer day . . . the souls of countless tribes and nations were flitting." He asked his father what was happening there and was told that they were the souls "destined to live in the body a second time" (Virgil, *The Aeneid,* Book VI, lines 688–720).

"Oh, Father, am I therefore to believe that of these souls some go, soaring hence, up to the world beneath our sky and return once more into dreary matter?" (Virgil, *The Aeneid,* Book VI, lines 688–720).

His father explained the cycle of existence and all the vast universe pervaded by spirit and mind. Everyone struggles in matter for a while, he said, and then finds the world of death fitted to himself. After the purification processes of the other world and when time's cycle is complete, the souls possess "a perception pure and bright, a spark of elemental fire" and are ready for the next cycle.

Anchises led his son to look down on the souls awaiting rebirth and told him the destiny of all who were to be of their own line. He forecast the founding of Rome and the spread of its great empire.

When it was time for Aeneas to go, though he had many questions still to ask, Anchises guided them to a place where they were faced by two gates. One was a gate of horn, "allowing an easy exit for shadows which are true." The other was of "shining white ivory," perfectly made, but through it the "spirits send visions which are false in the light of day" (Virgil, *The Aeneid,* Book VI, lines 879–901).

Anchises escorted his son and the sibyl with him to the gate of ivory.

✍ COMMENT ✍

J. G. Frazer, in his fat and famous book *The Golden Bough,* posits that the golden bough of Juno plucked by Aeneas is probably the same as that which grew in the groves of Diana at Nemi and was protected to the death by the king until a poor and ragged man managed to pick it and take the king's place as guardian of the grove and king of the land. He also posits that in both cases the bough in question is actually mistletoe growing high on the oak, in the branches. Mistletoe appears to have fallen from heaven when it is found growing on a sacred tree, and it grows apparently without reference to earth. It is the plant the ancient Celtic druids cut ritually with their golden knives, and it symbolized for them their most sacred beliefs. Some of us still hang mistletoe above the entrances to our homes at Christmas, the holiest time of the Christian year. We kiss those who pass under it, for it has come to denote harmony, love, and peace—the fresh start promised us by the Savior.

But whether it physically was mistletoe or not, the golden bough is symbolic of the passport we need before we can cross the frontiers of other realms. It is not enough that we demand a passport. We have to fulfill certain conditions and have the right credentials. The bough will not yield to any hand, but only to the one whom the powers that be have decided should have it. Aeneas was evidently worthy to have it, for the sibyl had called him a good and noble man. It came into his hand, and he and his guide entered the otherworld. Note that he did not go alone, even though he had the bough. His guide was the oracle of Cumae, an aged, aged woman steeped in the wisdom of centuries.

Readers of *The Aeneid* learn more about the oracle. On their return to the ordinary world, Aeneas in gratitude wanted to build her a temple. But she sighed and said she was mortal like himself and no human was worthy of holy incense. She then told him her story. Once she had been loved by Phoebus, who had offered her any gift she liked. She had asked to have as many years of life as there were grains of dust in a pile before them—but she forgot to ask for perpetual youth to go with her many years. She was therefore doomed to live year after year, generation after generation, growing older and older but not yet allowed to die.

Anchises told his son that everyone finds the world of death fitted to himself. This implies that there is no objective heaven and hell but only a state of being in which one either suffers the agonies of regret for what one has done on earth or experiences the happiness of having led a blameless and satisfying life. There seems to be no question of eternal punishment. When the souls are ready—when their "perception is pure and bright"—they return to earth. Apparently they remember their earthly existence when they are in the world of the dead but have to drink of the waters of Lethe, forgetfulness, when they return to earth. When Aeneas and the sibyl are ready to leave, they are sent back through the gate of ivory, the gate of false illusion, so that they will not remember exactly what they saw. Perhaps, like Hamlet, we are only prevented from committing suicide by the uncertainty of what we might find in "the undiscovered country, from whose bourne no traveller returns" (William Shakespeare, *Hamlet,* act 3, sc. 1).

Recently there has been a plethora of channelled books. So many that my husband, who was an editor and received many manuscripts purported to have been dictated by spirits of the dead, took to wearing a button that said, "Just because they're dead doesn't mean that they're smart." Though some of the books were wise, he was quite depressed that so many contradicted each other and so many were so foolish. We are not permitted to know what really happens after death for a very good reason, and we should not fight against it. It is the mystery, the uncertainty, that keeps us on our toes in this life. It may be the hope of something better that drives us on and the fear of something worse that induces us to make the most of what we have.

In my novel *The Winged Man* I suggest that the gate of horn is the gate through which we might encounter raw, untreated reality—that is, untreated in the sense of not having passed through the processes, both conscious and subconscious, devised by our minds to transform the vast and terrifying power of the universe into something we find more comfortable.

> Ahead they saw two gates—one plain and stark, carved of horn, and one elaborately carved of ivory. Neither appeared to be attached to any building but stood isolated in an otherwise empty field. The Sibyl was making for the further one—the one of ivory—but Bladud took the initiative this time and rushed to the nearer, the gate of horn. He heard her cry out that he should not go through—but he would not listen and flung it open.
>
> As he stepped onto the threshold he found himself being drawn into a vortex. The images he had recently seen whirled before him in a violent and confusing blur—transforming—becoming other—taking on their true meaning.

Sounds and visions too powerful to endure overwhelmed him. It was as though he were about to fall into the first chaos—the Void—the matrix of the worlds before order was conceived and the wild and boundless passions of the first energies were tamed. Terrified he clung to the door post, until the Sibyl reached for him and hauled him back.

"Not this one," she cried, "the other." She drew him, staggering and bewildered to the gate of ivory. Through this they entered the world as he had always known it—the nakedness of reality comfortably and safely clothed in illusion.

—Moyra Caldecott, *The Winged Man*

Sources of myth
Virgil, *The Aeneid*, Book VI.
Ovid, *Metamorphoses*, Book XIV.
J. G. Frazer, *The Golden Bough*.
Moyra Caldecott, *The Winged Man*.

The Oak of Dodona

Greek

Near the city of Dodona, in Epirus, there was a sacred grove of oaks that became one of the oldest and most respected oracular sites in ancient Greece. Some believed that the first temple was built there by Deucalian to celebrate his survival of the flood.

It is said that two black doves flew out of Egypt. One flew to Libya and the other to Dodona. Having alighted in the grove at Dodona, the bird began to speak in Greek with the voice of a woman, uttering many profound philosophical and religious truths and answering questions put to it. The grove became associated with Zeus, the supreme god of the Greek pantheon, and later with Jupiter, his Roman counterpart—but it was the dove out of Egypt that spoke, and it was the priests of Zeus who listened. The men and women who came to the grove, seeking the oracle, brought offerings and stood in awe beneath the mighty tree, hearing the rustling of the leaves as the dove moved about, fearfully waiting for the priests to pass on what she said.

Later, the first priesthood of the grove, the Selloi, mysteriously disappeared, and their successors, three priestesses who were not so adept at interpreting the words of the dove, instituted a bronze vase, which when struck vibrated with sound for hours. The vase

was placed on a column among the trees. Beside it was a statue of a child who held a whip with many cords. Each cord was finished with a tiny metal ball. When the wind blew, the balls bounced against the hollow bronze vase, setting up a cacophony of sound. And this became the voice of the oracle for many centuries.

꧁ COMMENT ꧂

It is significant that the dove came from Egypt, because Egyptian civilization was already ancient when Greek civilization was in its infancy. Egyptian wisdom, Egyptian magic, Egyptian skill with stone, with medicine, with practically everything was highly prized by the Greeks. Greek wise men prided themselves on the learning they had brought from Egypt. Plato's description of the golden age of Atlantis and its ultimate destruction has caught the imagination of the world. It is said that there are more than three thousand books about Atlantis in the world today, and many people who believe in reincarnation believe they have lived in ancient times in Atlantis. Plato claims to have received the information about Atlantis from Solon, who in turn received it from the Egyptian priesthood.

Why are the doves black instead of white? In Egypt, from whence the doves came, black was the color of life. The life-giving silt that lay on the fields the whole length of the Nile valley after the annual inundation had passed, and on which the fertility of Egypt depended, was black. Now, with the Aswan Dam, the inundation does not come, and the rich and important silt does not regenerate the fields each year.

The dove from Egypt does not speak alone as oracle. The dove rustles the leaves of the great oak tree, and it is from this combination of bird and tree that the priests take the messages. The bird represents the spirit infused with the ancient wisdom of Egypt, while the tree represents the growing, developing new wisdom of Greece. Neither one nor the other is enough by itself.

I can't help thinking that when the dove first landed in the tree, someone—perhaps a herd-boy resting in the shade—heard the rustling and believed it was a voice. Possibly the voice came not from the tree at all but from his own higher self, encouraged to speak out as so often happens when we are in relaxed and peaceful surroundings. I believe he heard true and needed no interpreter. But then as time went by and crowds came to the tree on hearing his story, the usual thing happened. Someone took charge. Someone organized the whole thing. Priests were given the power to interpret and mediate. In our own day we have seen how Lourdes is no longer a place where one can commune in silence with nature and with the queen of heaven, and I'm sure that around the oak at Dodona there soon grew up the same razzmatazz of crowds and people selling things. To me it is significant that the dove stopped speaking and the tree stopped rustling and a new priesthood had to invent a more obvious and mechanical way of "hearing" the voices of the gods to keep the lucrative flow of offerings going.

There are many precedents for trees as sacred oracles and historical monuments.

Alexander the Great, travelling northward in India, is reputed to have consulted two oracle trees. "No sacrifices are allowed in the holy grove where they stand: Alexander kisses the bark of the Tree of the Sun and, as he is instructed, formulates his question only in his mind. The Tree of the Sun begins to answer him in the language of India and ends its message in Greek. Then he has to wait for night fall to consult the Tree of the Moon. Again he kisses the bark of the tree and formulates his question. As moonlight falls on its silver leaves this tree begins to speak first in Greek and then in the Indian tongue. The messages from both trees are doom-laden: he will never return home, he will die poisoned through the treachery of one of his companions, his mother will perish miserably. In the morning he is allowed to consult a naked tree on the top of which the Phoenix nests. The answers are no kinder" (William Anderson, *Green Man*, pp. 32–33).

Shakespeare refers in *As You Like It* to trees as "counsellors that feelingly persuade me who I am."

Abraham first met Jehovah under a sacred oak tree at Sechem. Absalom hung on a sacred oak between heaven and earth.

The oak is solid, dependable, durable. It grows to a great age and spreads its branches wide. The great oak forests of ancient times would naturally lend themselves to thoughts of magic and mystery. Behind a door of oak we are safe in our world of ordinary objects and events, but through it we glimpse the splendors and terrors of the unknown. Dare we step through? To the Jews the oak was the tree of the covenant, the divine presence (J. C. Cooper, *An Illustrated Encyclopaedia of Traditional Symbols,* p. 121). I see the kabbalists' tree of life always as an oak.

Under the Gospel Oak at Parliament Hill, Hampstead, London, Edward the Confessor declared for Christianity. Under an oak, still visible today in Kent between Holwood Farm and Keston, William Wilberforce had the inspiration to oppose slavery and change the course of history: "At length I well remember after a conversation with Mr. Pitt in the open air at the root of an old tree at Holwood just above the steep descent into the vale of Keston I resolved to give notice on a fit occasion in the House of Commons of my intention to bring forward the abolition of the slave trade" (*Diary,* 1787).

"The ancient oak of Guernica is a most venerable ancient monument," says William Wordsworth in his prelude to his poem on the subject. "Ferdinand and Isabella, in the year 1476, after hearing mass in the church of Santa Maria de la Antigua, repaired to this tree, under which they swore to the Biscayans to maintain their privileges." The "Oak of Guernica" is dated 1810 and mourns the loss of these freedoms:

> *Oak of Guernica! Tree of holier power*
> *Than that which in Dodona did enshrine*
> *(So faith too fondly deemed) a voice divine*
> *Heard from the depths of its aerial bower —*
> *How canst thou flourish at this blighting hour?*
> . . .
> *If never more within their shady round*
> *Those lofty-minded Lawgivers shall meet,*
> *Peasant and lord, in their appointed seat,*
> *Guardians of Biscay's ancient liberty.*

Sources of myth

William Anderson, *Green Man: The Archetype of Our Oneness with the Earth.*
J. C. Cooper, *An Illustrated Encyclopaedia of Traditional Symbols.*
Larousse Encyclopaedia of Mythology.
Manly P. Hall, *The Secret Teachings of All Ages.*
William Wilberforce, *Diary.*

The Dream of Nebuchadnezzar

Hebrew

After the destruction of the Assyrian Empire, the Babylonians under Nebuchadnezzar II (604–562 B.C.E.) became extremely powerful. They repulsed an attack by the Egyptian Pharaoh Necho II in 601 and destroyed the nation of Judah in 597, sacking and burning Jerusalem, looting the great temple, torturing and blinding King Zedekiah, and carrying off many people into exile. Among these were Daniel, Hananiah, Mishael, and Azariah, renamed by Nebuchadnezzar Belteshazzar, Shadrach, Meshach, and Abed-Nego.

Nebuchadnezzar believed there was nothing he could not do. He had a huge and magnificent palace, his empire stretched far and wide from the Lower Sea (the Persian Gulf) to the Great Sea (the Mediterranean), and he had the power of life and death over thousands upon thousands of people.

But one night he had a dream, and the dream frightened him. He called all the wise men of Babylon to him—the magicians, the astrologers, the diviners, and the soothsayers—and told them what he had dreamed, demanding an explanation. But not one of them could offer a satisfactory interpretation.

He then remembered the wisdom of Daniel (Belteshazzar), one of the Hebrews he had captured in the sack of Jerusalem, who had

already interpreted dreams and proved his extraordinary abilities.

Nebuchadnezzar told Daniel what he had dreamed. He had seen an enormous tree growing in the middle of the earth, its roots deep and its branches as high as heaven. From its fruit all men ate. In its shade all beasts rested. On its twigs all birds sang.

Then, as he dreamed, it seemed to him a holy being, who had been watching the tree from heaven, approached and demanded that it be hewn down, its branches stripped off, and its leaves and fruit shaken and scattered. The birds flew away. The beasts moved off. Only the stump was left, bound with iron and brass. All its mighty splendor was gone, and it was no higher than the lowliest beast of the field.

"Let his heart be changed from man's, and let a beast's heart be given into him; and let seven times pass over him." This decree was given in the dream by those who watch—the holy ones of the Most High.

"For the Most High," they said, "ruleth the kingdom of men, and He giveth kingship to whomsoever he will, and no one may question Him."

Then Nebuchadnezzar pleaded with Daniel to interpret the dream, but Daniel frowned and was puzzled. He thought long and hard and at last warned the king that the interpretation would be more likely to please his enemies than himself. But Nebuchadnezzar insisted on hearing what Daniel had to say.

"The mighty tree that grew so high and strong, Majesty, is you who rule over the lives of men, who feed and give shelter to millions, whom no man can discomfort. But the Lord Almighty, the Most High, ruleth over all, even you, and it is He who decrees who shall have and who shall have not—even to the kingdom of men, even to the throne in your palace. The cutting down of the tree shows that you will lose your great power and privilege and status and will become no better than a beast of the field, wet with the dew at night, tearing at the grass for food by day, having no honor among men. Seven times shall pass before you will accept that the Most High, and no man, is the ruler of men, and it is in His power and in His power only that man has or has not. But because in the dream the stump and the roots of the tree were left in the ground, it will be possible for you to regain your kingdom if the Most High so pleases."

Nebuchadnezzar the king listened to Daniel and was disturbed by his prophecy. But as the days passed and nothing changed in his life he began to forget the warning he had received.

A year later, walking in his palace, every man bowing to the ground before him, he looked around him and was proud of the might of Babylon and the power he had over the lives of men. But even as he boasted of his achievements—the wealth and honor of his great kingdom, the seven-tiered ziggurat that reached to heaven, the beautiful terraced gardens, the avenues guarded by sculpted lions, the ramparts and elegant houses of a city more luxurious than any before—he thought he heard a voice saying, "O Nebuchadnezzar, King of Babylon, thy kingdom is departed from thee."

He turned to see who had spoken, but no one was there.

Everything was changed. He was naked, on his hands and knees in the red dust of the wilderness. He could think of nothing but his hunger and his thirst. Whereas once he had sipped the choicest wines out of golden goblets, now he lapped like an animal at a muddy water hole. Once he had eaten white meat and red garnished with the finest sauces; now he tore at the sparse blades of grass and was glad of the sustenance they provided. Thoughts came and went, strangely disconnected—flashes of memory lost in fog, nothing making sense. He tried to speak, but the words that had come so easily before would not come to him now. Only sounds that a beast would make came from him. His hair grew like eagle's feathers and his nails like claws.

He lost track of time, but in the city of Babylon the people mourned the terrible madness that had destroyed their king. Slavering and slobbering and gabbling incoherently, he had been driven from the city gates.

But one day he returned, walking upright. He had washed himself in the river. He was clad in a lion's skin. His eyes were clear. His speech was strong and sure. The people fell at his feet and welcomed him home.

Nebuchadnezzar had learned how uncertain and insecure man's hold on even the kingdom of himself can be. He knew now he held the kingdom of Babylon only as the gift of the Most High "whose dominion is an everlasting dominion, and whose kingdom is from generation to generation."

"All honor to the King of Heaven," he declared, "all whose works are truth, and His ways judgment. Those who walk in pride He is able to debase. None can stay His hand, or say unto Him, what doest thou?"

~ COMMENT ~

This time the interpretation or commentary is given within the story, and I would not presume to argue with it. A few points are worth noting, however.

This was not Nebuchadnezzar's first brush with the Jewish God. Some time earlier, he had made an immense image of gold, before which he had insisted all in his kingdom should bow down. The three Jews he had renamed Shadrach, Meshach, and Abed-Nego refused to bow to the idol, and in his rage Nebuchadnezzar had flung them into a fiery furnace. (Daniel must have been elsewhere at that time, for he is not mentioned, and it is certain he also would have refused such a command.)

There, in the fiery furnace, Nebuchadnezzar had seen the three Jews, accompanied by an angel, talking and walking as though they were in no discomfort at all. Awed by the power of the Jewish God, Nebuchadnezzar had called the three men out of the fire and spoken these words: "Blessed be the God of Shadrach, Meshach, and Abed-Nego, who hath sent his angel, and delivered his servants that trusted in him, and have changed the king's word, and yielded their bodies, that they might not serve nor worship any god, except their own God" (Daniel 3:28).

But time passed and Nebuchadnezzar forgot.

The lesson Nebuchadnezzar learned could be expressed as simply as in the old adage "pride goes before a fall" or with more complexity as expressed by Roger Cook in *The Tree of Life:* "Daniel interpreted this tree as representing the king himself who, in modern psychological terms, had identified his limited and personal self with the divine Selfhood which his kingship symbolized. It was this that finally brought about his madness . . . and he regressed to the level of a beast of the field" (p. 109).

Nebuchadnezzar faced a perennial question, one that has troubled thinkers since the remotest times. Do we have free will, or are we completely under the power of a controlling force?

The Gnostic Gospels found in 1945 at Nag Hammadi in Egypt and dating back to the very earliest centuries after Christ, the Cathars in medieval France, the Hermeticists in Renaissance Italy, and even today the "New Age" movement in the United States and Britain—all claim that a person by his or her own efforts can rise through "gnosis," or the direct experience of sublime truths, to a state where he or she is absorbed into the deity and indeed returns to the oneness from which he or she originally came. It is a concept not unlike the state of nirvana described by the Buddhists. Mainstream theologians in the Christian tradition, however, declare this to be heresy and say that nothing can be gained by one's own efforts, everything depending on the grace of the deity. Admittedly, Nebuchadnezzar did not claim mystic union with God in the spiritual sense, for he operated at that time on a much lower level, not realizing there is anything beyond worldly power. Only after the most frightening lesson—the loss of his mind and of his power to think, reason, and remember—did he notice that what he had had, an empire, was nothing in the greater scheme of things.

The Gnostics' admiration of man's innate divinity is based on the excitement we all feel when we notice how our minds can encompass the universe. Nothing seems too difficult for us to imagine, and nothing too impossible for us to invent or control—except, in fact, the ultimate mystery: God.

It is noteworthy that Nebuchadnezzar lost his kingdom because he lost his mind. Without a mind we cannot operate in the world. Without a mind, what are we? But the roots of the tree were not destroyed. Nebuchadnezzar's soul was left, and from his soul another "tree" could grow.

Nebuchadnezzar had to learn that "suffering is the result of the Immortal Man's falling in love with his shadow and giving up Reality to dwell in the darkness of illusion" as Hermes Trismegistus says in *The Divine Pomander* (quoted in Manly P. Hall, *The Secret Teachings of All Ages*, p. xxxix).

Nebuchadnezzar had thought that worldly power was important, that his mind was important. He suffered when they were taken from him. He learned that there was something more enduring than a mighty empire, than even the mind of man—the mystery of the holy word that no one can spoil because no one but God himself can know it.

I feel that Nebuchadnezzar before his madness was a worldly conqueror and his god a golden statute, but after his recovery he was more concerned with the mysteries of an immaterial god. When he walked the spiral path around the seven-tiered garden in his palace grounds that was fed by a cascade of water from a pool at the pyramidal top—so famous they later became known as the hanging gardens of Babylon and were named as one of the seven wonders of the ancient world—he saw his progress as the progress of the soul through the seven levels of reality, each level nourished from above, from the highest source he had encountered in the wilderness: the "dark night of the soul" that often seems so necessary for spiritual growth. Similarly, the ziggurat no longer reached merely to the sun we see in the sky, but beyond it to the light beyond all light—the ultimate and most high.

Sources of myth
    The Bible: Daniel 4:1-37.
    Roger Cook, *The Tree of Life.*
    John Baines and Jaromír Málek, *Atlas of Ancient Egypt.*
    Reader's Digest Atlas of the Bible.

The Two Trees of Eden

Hebrew

And the Lord God planted a garden eastward in Eden; and there he put the man whom he had formed. And out of the ground made the Lord God to grow every tree that is pleasant to the sight, and good for food; the tree of life also in the midst of the garden, and the tree of knowledge of good and evil. . . .

And the Lord God took the man, and put him in the garden of Eden to dress it and to keep it.

And the Lord God commanded the man saying: Of every tree of the garden thou mayest freely eat: but of the tree of the knowledge of good and evil, thou shalt not eat of it: for in the day that thou eatest thereof thou shalt surely die.

After that God made every "beast of the field" and "fowl of the air" and called upon the man to name them. Then God created Eve out of the rib of Adam and called her "woman." "And they were both naked, the man and his wife, and were not ashamed."

But the serpent, "more subtle than any beast of the field," persuaded Eve to take the fruit of the forbidden tree of the knowledge of good and evil. She ate and persuaded her husband to eat, and "the eyes of them both were opened, and they knew that they

were naked. . . . And they heard the voice of the Lord God walking in the garden in the cool of the day: and Adam and his wife hid themselves from the presence of the Lord amongst the trees of the garden."

The Lord found them and questioned them. He was angry and told them the consequences of their action: "In sorrow shalt thou eat of it all the days of thy life." And he drove them from Eden lest they put forth their hands, "and take also of the tree of life, and eat, and live forever."

"Behold, the man has become as one of us, knowing good and evil."

"He placed at the east of the garden of Eden Cherubims, and a flaming sword which turned every way, to keep the way of the tree of life."

⚘ COMMENT ⚘

The Tree of Knowledge

The story of the tree of knowledge is layered with meaning. One interpretation could be that it is a mythic representation of humankind's imperfection—the tragic loss of full potential because of impatience. At the time Adam and Eve plucked and ate, they were not worthy or ready to do so, and the consciousness of life they gained by eating too soon of the fruit brought only pain and confusion. The unfoldment of knowledge, the careful mastering of one mystery before moving on to the next that was part of the original and beautiful plan, would have led us at last to the perfect point of conscious union with our God. But it was lost when man and woman thought they knew better than God and grabbed impatiently for something beyond their reach.

Many people do not accept literally that a couple who disobeyed a precise instruction from God four thousand or forty thousand years ago brought about a punishment that has tormented generation upon generation of millions of people. It may well be truer that Adam and Eve represent us as we are every day of our lives and that we have the choice at every moment of obeying the great and necessary laws of God or of breaking them. If we break them, we are "driven from paradise" and have a long and difficult struggle to get back. If we obey them, we fulfill our potential and are happy "in paradise" here and now. This principle holds on all levels, from the mundane and material, where we risk the desert if we cut down all the forests and live in perpetual fear of nuclear holocaust because we ate yet another fruit of the tree of knowledge before we were (morally) ready to digest it, to the sublime, where we suffer when we deny our divine origin and the realms beyond the material, thus limiting ourselves and missing out on great and wonderful possibilities.

That God has given us free will in order to make us worthy companions, and yet has put precise and terrible prohibitions on certain things and actions, at first seems puzzling and unfair. But any of us who have had difficult passages in our lives—who have had to struggle against pain and adversity and have found that in the end we are wiser and spiritually richer for the experience—will understand that a bland freedom in which everything is perfect is extraordinarily enervating and stultifying. We wonder whether the "disobedience" of Adam and Eve was not written into the original blueprint as being the only way to introduce the necessary friction into the situation—the necessary challenge and dynamism. The long and bitter "punishment" may not be a punishment at all but an opportunity for growth and fulfillment.

The Tree of Life

The tree of life stands at the beginning, in the first book of the Bible, and at the end, in the last book: in Eden and in the New Jerusalem. It stands wherever we are, though more often than not we do not recognize it. Yet we ignore it at our peril. It represents not only life itself, but the source of life, the Mystery beyond mysteries, the One which diversified but which wishes ultimately to return to being One.

> I am Alpha and Omega, the beginning and the end, the first and the last. Blessed are they that do his commandments, that they may have right to the tree of life, and may enter in through the gates of the city (Revelation 22: 13-14).

> Christ is sacrificed at the centre of the world, on the Cosmic Tree, which stretches from heaven to earth and stands at the midpoint of the horizontal radial cross of the four directions . . .

It is related to the Tree of Life at the Centre of the Garden of Eden at the beginning of time and at the centre of the Heavenly City of Jerusalem at the end of time. . . . It is Alpha and Omega—the beginning and the end (Roger Cook, *The Tree of Life*, p. 20).

The tree of life, rooted in the centre of god's garden, expands through the ages and finally bursts through the limitations of cyclic time into end-time. For the tree planted in Eden, at earth's sacred centre, is destined for final realization in the sacred centre of heavenly Jerusalem. The tree is drawn up through time and then passes out of time, into eternity by way of the cross, the crux, the passage point. Christ, Beginning and End, binds the two realities, the two sacred places (Meinrad Craighead, *The Sign of the Tree*, p. 38).

The early Church Fathers recognized the world tree as the specific symbol of the cross, the true tree of life. It is often said that the early Church baptized much deep-rooted religious thought; the many customs and rituals which attracted the first Christians conditioned them culturally and psychologically. Certainly in the first Christian centuries the Fathers of both East and West knew that the sign of the cosmic tree was familiar to their people. Origen, Hippolytus, John Chrysostom, and Augustine, for example, interpreted this sign and amplified its meaning, referring to the cross as "an immortal plant," "pillar of the universe," "bond of all things," and "centre of the cosmos." They thus led their people to understand in imagery their recognition of the cross tree as a consummation of the cosmic tree which betokened it (Meinrad Craighead, *The Sign of the Tree*, p. 34).

This tree, wide as the heavens itself, has grown up into heaven from the earth. It is an immortal growth and towers between heaven and earth. It is the fulcrum of all things and the place where they are all at rest. It is the foundation of the round world, the center of the cosmos. In it all the diversities in our human nature are formed into unity. It is held together by the invisible nails of the spirit so that it may not break loose from the divine. It touches the highest summits of heaven and makes the earth firm beneath its foot, and it grasps the middle regions between them with immeasurable arms (Hippolytus, Bishop of Rome, Easter sermon, third century).

Under the appellations of the *Tree of Life* and the *Tree of Knowledge of Good and Evil* is concealed the great arcanum of antiquity—the mystery of equilibrium. The Tree of Life represents the spiritual point of balance—the secret of immortality. The Tree of Knowledge of Good and Evil, as its name implies, represents polarity, or unbalance—the secret of mortality. The Qabbalists reveal this by assigning the central column of their sephirothic diagram to the Tree of Life and the two side branches to the Tree of Knowledge of Good and Evil (Manly P. Hall, *The Secret Teachings of All Ages,* p. xcv).

In many cases the center is conceived as an axis extending vertically to the pole star and downward to some pivotal point in the abyss. Iconographically, it may be represented as a mountain, a stairway or ladder, a pole, or very commonly a tree. It is symbolized in our Christmas tree, with the pivotal star at its summit, bounteous gifts appearing beneath, and the Christ child, greatest gift of all, in the creche at its base; while below, as we may imagine, are its roots in the fiery abyss. But equally it is symbolized in the Cross (Joseph Campbell, *The Mythic Image,* II: 90).

We find the symbols that are deployed so powerfully in the Biblical story occurring time and again in different and often earlier mythologies. In Greek mythology the fearsome snake guarded the precious golden apples on the mystical island of the Hesperides. Roger Cook mentions in *The Tree of Life* that in ancient Babylon the Tree of Truth and the Tree of Life were believed to stand at the eastern entrance to heaven (p. 24). Joseph Campbell describes in *Occidental Mythology* the symbol of the four rivers flowing to the four directions from the central sacred tree on a Syro-Hittite seal featuring the hero Gilgamesh (p. 12). In the Hawaiian Islands, "the tree of eternal life and the tree which brings knowledge of death are pictured as one." "One side of this tree is alive and green, the other dead, dry, and brittle" (Roger Cook, *The Tree of Life,* p. 24).

In Minoan Crete, many seal rings depict the sacred tree. From Egypt we find the following in the Pyramid Texts, some of the earliest known texts in the world: "There is an island in the marsh of offerings over which stars fly like swallows. Herein is the *Tree of Life*" (S. A. B. Mercer, *Pyramid Texts,* 1216 a–c).

In northern Europe, the maypole dance in spring and the Christmas tree in winter hark back to the sacred trees of pagan times. Later religions often transformed the symbols of an earlier discarded religion that were so potent they could not be ignored into symbols that worked for them. One Christian legend tells of how "Mary and Jesus took refuge in the holy tree of Mataria, the sycamore of Isis-Hathor, Goddess of Dendera" (Budge, *Gods of the Egyptians,* Vol. 2, p. 220).

Sources of myth

The Bible, Genesis 2 and 3; Revelation 22.
Roger Cook, *The Tree of Life.*
Meinrad Craighead, *The Sign of the Tree.*
Joseph Campbell, *The Mythic Image* and *The Masks of God.*
Barbara G. Walker, *The Woman's Encyclopaedia of Myths and Secrets.*
H. R. Ellis Davidson, *Scandinavian Mythology.*
Manly P. Hall, *The Secret Teachings of All Ages.*
E. A. Wallis Budge, *Gods of the Egyptians.*
S. A. B. Mercer, *Pyramid Texts,* Vol. 4, 1216 a–c.

Eve's Tree of Redemption

Western European/Christian

I n the first shock of realizing that she had brought down the wrath of Jehovah on their heads and that she and Adam were to be driven in disgrace from the Garden of Eden because of her disobedience, Eve hardly noticed that she still carried the twig with which the fatal apple had been attached to the tree of the knowledge of good and evil.

Adam and Eve began their wanderings in exile. At last they chose to settle in one place, where Eve, finding that the twig was still as fresh and green as it was when first plucked from the tree, planted it in the ground. Almost immediately the twig quickened and took root. Eve, gazing tearfully at the reminder of how much she had lost by her thoughtless action, watered it with her penitential tears, and it grew swiftly into a tall and slender tree.

In all its glory it was as white as snow. Its trunk, its branches, and its leaves were all white.

One day Adam and Eve were sitting in its shade, bewailing their fate and calling the tree they sat under the "tree of death," for the plucking of it had brought suffering and death into the world.

Suddenly they heard a voice telling them that the tree had more of life in it than death. They believed this was the voice of their

God and interpreted the words to mean that through this tree they would somehow be redeemed.

At this they rejoiced. They took cuttings from the tree and planted them wherever they could. Each new planting grew and flourished, and each was as white and pure as the parent tree.

One day Adam and Eve were sitting in its shade again when they heard the voice of their God commanding them to unite as man and wife. Somewhat startled by the command, they looked at each other. Almost immediately a dark fog appeared and enveloped them so that they could not see each other. Through this fog they reached for each other, and eventually they touched and made love. From that coupling their first-born, Abel, was conceived.

When the fog lifted, Adam and Eve could see that the tree was no longer white, but green in wood and leaf and bark. In its new green form it flourished and for the first time bore blossom and fruit. All the cuttings Adam and Eve planted from it were also green and bore blossom and fruit.

Their son Abel grew to be a virtuous and noble man. He offered to the Lord "the first-fruits of the finest things he had," while his brother, Cain, a very different type of man, "took the scurviest and worst part of his harvest to offer to his Maker." Cain hated Abel because he could find no fault with him, and consequently his own faults were more noticeable by contrast. One day, while Abel was resting in the shade of the tree, Cain slew him and buried him beneath the tree.

The tree underwent one more transformation to mark this event. Its hue was now red, the color of blood. No cutting from it thrived, but all withered and died when they were put in the earth.

Years passed and the population of the earth multiplied, behaving with such wickedness that Jehovah ordered storms and floods to wash away the filth.

⚘ COMMENT ⚘

The story is another "spin-off" legend from the garden of Eden story. This time Eve receives reassurance that eventually her sin will be forgiven and that the spark of life they had before the Fall might well kindle again.

In the Adam story, three trees are involved (see next story); in this case there is actually only one tree, but three phases of their human existence are marked symbolically by changes in the tree.

The anonymous, early-thirteenth-century author who retold this ancient legend in his collection of stories *The Quest for the Holy Grail* takes care to point out that the changes of color mark important turning points in the spiritual life of mankind. With the first color, white, he draws a careful distinction between maidenhood and virginity. Adam and Eve had no doubt performed the sex act since their flight from Eden, but according to the medieval author she was still a virgin when she planted the twig. "Maidenhood," he writes, "is a virtue common to those of either sex who have not known the contact born of carnal commerce. But virginity is something infinitely higher and more worth; for none, whether man or woman, can possess it who has inclined in will to carnal intercourse. Such virginity did Eve still have when she was driven out of Paradise and the delights it held: nor had she lost this virtue at the time of the branch's planting." That is why the first tree is white and pure. One *chooses* to be a virgin, whereas maidenhood is a state without choice. Is the author saying Eve chose to be a virgin after those first unwitting attempts at sex after eating the apple? With their God's new directive they enter a new phase: sex is no longer an instinctive activity natural to animals but somehow shameful to humans; it is to be graced. In a real and lasting relationship, with God's approval, the sex act is a unifying act that means one is no longer alone (separate, virginal). At this point, significantly, the tree becomes green and verdant. The black fog perhaps symbolizes the change in Adam and Eve since the Fall—they now obey him blindly, accepting that whatever he tells them to do or not to do is part of his mighty plan for the world. Their obedience in this instance starts the process toward redemption. The tree has reached its full natural potential. It is green and flourishing; it blossoms and fruits. Eve bears a child. The earth burgeons.

But Cain's jealousy and the foul deed of fratricide turns the tree red. Cuttings from it wither and die.

The issue is not just the murder but Cain's selfishness and greed in not sending to God what was required. That someone should offer the finest of his or her "first-fruits" to the Lord does not limit the concept to a farmer laying his finest calf on an altar. In its wider context, it means that all our best efforts—all our creative genius and our skills and talents—should be aimed at the highest and noblest idea of the Divine we can conceive. Cain represents those of us who live only by our lowest and basest impulses, whose selfishness and greed is rapidly creating a wasteland of our world.

Although the fruit has traditionally been called an apple, it might well have been a quince. Robert Temple points this out in his translation of the ancient Sumerian epic of Gilgamesh (p. 97, note 14), saying it was not likely that apples would be growing in the Middle East at that time.

Sources of myth
P. M. Matarasso, trans. *The Quest for the Holy Grail.*
Robert Temple, trans. *He Who Saw Everything: A Verse Translation of the Epic of Gilgamesh.*

Adam's Tree of Redemption

Western European/Christian

When Adam felt that he was near to death, he called his son Seth to him—Seth, the son Eve had conceived to take the place of Abel whom Cain had murdered; Seth, begotten in the likeness of Adam, after his own image; Seth, who was the son of Adam, who was the son of God.

"Go to paradise, my son," Adam said to Seth, "and fetch me the oil of mercy that I may be anointed before my death, for the burden of my sins weigh heavy on me."

Seth set off and retraced his father's steps toward Eden. At first he passed through a bleak and desolate landscape, where no green shoots grew and no beast stirred. Then he began to hear music and see grass and flowers. His pace quickened, but before he could enter the gate to Eden his way was barred by the mighty figure of the archangel Mik-hael, wielding a sword of flame.

"The time has not yet come for reopening the gates of paradise," the archangel said. "But the tree that grows from Adam's grave will bear his redeemer. Step forward, Seth," he continued. "You may look three times into paradise, though you may not enter."

Eagerly Seth stepped forward and looked through the gates of paradise. There he saw a garden more beautiful than any he could

have imagined. At the confluence of four rivers, his eye was caught by the image of a bare and shattered tree.

"Take another look," the archangel said.

This time Seth saw the serpent coiled around its trunk. He noticed that the tree was growing above an abyss. His brother Cain was struggling in the roots to free himself, but some roots even penetrated his flesh.

Horrified, he looked away, and when he looked back for the third time he saw a green and spreading tree with a beautiful woman in its branches, a laughing child upon her knee. Seven white doves were circling above the crown of the tree.

Mik-hael told Seth that this child would save the world from Adam's sin. He then gave Adam's son three seeds from the fruit of the tree.

"Three days after your return home, your father will die. When he does, place these three seeds upon his tongue," he told Seth.

Seth returned to his father and told him all that had occurred. Adam died happy, and from his body three trees grew: a cypress, a pine, and a cedar. They twined about each other to make one tree—the most magnificent that anyone had ever seen.

From this tree were fashioned the miraculous rod of Moses, the flowering rod of Aaron, and the pillars of the Temple of Solomon.

And from the wood of this tree the Romans made the cross of Christ.

COMMENT

Evidently God cannot yet bring himself to forgive the disobedience of Adam and Eve outright, but he does soften the situation by letting Adam know before he dies that mankind will eventually be forgiven through the intercession and sacrifice of His own son, the new Adam. The redemption will grow out of the old Adam himself, so what he had started he will finish. The messenger Seth who bears the good news is the "new" Abel.

As in so many myths, the number three features significantly: Adam, Eve, the snake; purity, temptation, fall; sin, penance, forgiveness. Seth looks into paradise three times. He sees three visions: the tree destroyed by sin, the process of penance, the forgiveness. He bears home three seeds, out of which three trees grow—but the three trees become one as the Trinity of Father, Son, and Holy Ghost is one.

Seeds may be planted but they do not always grow. They are potential, not actual. The soil of Adam's soul must be ready for the seed. God judges that it is so.

Three trees grow: the cypress, the pine, the cedar.

According to J. C. Cooper, the cypress is both a phallic symbol and a symbol of death. It represents the first tree Seth saw—the tree associated with Adam's concupiscence. The pine represents strength of character and uprightness—the years during which Adam tried to live according to God's law to make up for what he had done. The cedar represents nobility, incorruptibility, majesty, stateliness, and beauty. Its sacred wood was used for Solomon's temple. Here, no doubt, it represents the Christ.

William Anderson mentions this story in his interesting study of the occurrences of the image of an ancient fertility god, the Green Man, in Christian churches through the ages. New religions often use images from the religions they supersede, borrowing their potency and strength to emphasize a new and different point they want to make. The carved image of the pagan green god with leaves growing from his mouth has become, in the Gothic cathedral and the humble parish church, the symbol of God's forgiveness and the redemption of man through the living Christ. Such images are often tucked away almost out of sight in British and European Gothic cathedrals and village churches. As the United States did not have the Gothic period of architecture, it is possible that these secret remnants of the ancient earth religion were not incorporated into American churches. But any visitor to Europe might well enjoy seeking them out.

Adam lies dying, but from his body, as from the body of the Egyptian god Osiris, plants grow. Death is not a finality, as the seasonal renewal of vegetation has reminded humankind since the beginning. In the story of Adam, Seth, and the three trees, this natural phenomenon takes on added significance.

Sources of myth
   Roger Cook, *The Tree of Life: Meditations in Images and Words.*
   Meinrad Craighead, *The Sign of the Tree: The Archetype of Our Oneness with the Earth.*
   William Anderson, *Green Man.*

133

The Woman Who Was Turned into a Tree

African/Bushman

There were twenty sisters who went down to the river in the heat of the day, took off their clothes, and played in the water. A man came by who had eyes in his feet. He sat down on the dress of one of them and watched them at play. He said, "If she who owns this dress wants it back, she must bring me thorns." The woman whose dress it was brought him thorns. He took them from her and stuck them in her flesh. Then he lifted her and flung her in the air. When she came down she was a thorn tree rooted in the earth.

Her sisters, seeing what had happened to her, fled, and no matter how desperately she called them they would not come back.

Then one day Heiseb, the god who walks among people, came to the place and heard the tree calling. He commanded the woman to come forth from the tree—and she came. He asked her where her nineteen sisters were, and she did not know, for they had fled from her.

Heiseb saw a bull approaching and told the young woman to grasp the horns of the bull to discern where her sisters had gone. She was afraid but followed his suggestion and grasped the bull by the horns. Instantly she knew where she would find her sisters.

Heiseb asked whether she would be all right to go alone in search of them, but she asked that he accompany her, for she was still afraid.

So Heiseb and the woman came at last to where her sisters dwelt, and Heiseb asked where the man was who had changed their sister into a tree. They did not know and asked him, who knew all things, to tell them where he was.

Heiseb suggested that one of them should take off her dress and lay it down while he and the others kept watch.

Sure enough, the man approached and sat down on the dress. When he demanded thorns for the release of the dress, Heiseb showed himself.

"Thorns we have none, good friend, but here is that which is sharper than thorns."

And he drove his spear through the man's heart.

~ COMMENT ~

One interpretation of this story is clearly sexual, it seems to me. The man has eyes in his feet, not in his head; that is, he sees only with his lower self, not his higher. He watches the naked girls and forces one to make love to him. In Africa thorns are long and dangerous. Even in English-speaking countries a penis is often called a "prick."

The young woman cannot go with her sisters after the act. Her life has changed. She is restricted, shamed, and shunned. The rape has changed her and locked her into a state of hopeless inaction.

The god sees her plight and helps her. It is important that before she can return to her family and her normal life, she has to grasp the horns of a bull. She has to face the bull and take control. She has to accept what has happened to her and fearlessly grasp the power of the sexual act for herself.

The god punishes the man, but the women who had deserted their sister have to play a role in capturing him.

The story can also be read as an allegory of the man's spiritual progress. He has his eyes in his feet; that is, he can see no further than his immediate physical surroundings. He demands thorns of the spiritual beings he sees in the river of life, thus wasting a wonderful opportunity for spiritual advancement. He has no conception of what spiritual riches he could have from his encounter with the spirit-women; perhaps if he had asked and not demanded, the whole scenario might have been different. As it is, he aggressively seizes what he wants and by doing so brings about a kind of stalemate. He wanders on, unregenerate, and is caught by making the same mistake again.

Why are there twenty sisters? According to J. C. Cooper, in *An Illustrated Encyclopaedia of Traditional Symbols* (p. 120), twenty is the number symbolic of "the whole man" because it is the sum of all our fingers and toes. The women in the river constitute a whole. The man takes away part of the whole. Disunity, discordance, destruction follows. Only in the reuniting of the sisters in a common aim to destroy their destroyer is wholeness restored.

What is sharper than a thorn? Sudden revelation. The spear pierces the man's heart.

Source of myth
   E. W. Thomas, *Bushman Stories.*

Two Sisters

African/Kenyan

There were once two sisters. One made pots and the other did the housework. One day the girl who did the housework became angry that she had all the boring work to do while the other had the joy of making pots. Angrily she smashed the pots of her sister.

The girl whose beautiful pots were smashed ran away from home and wandered in the wilderness for three days. On the third day she came to a lake, in the center of which was a tree. She longed to reach the tree, but it was too far away and the lake water was cold and deep.

The tree moved nearer and nearer to the girl at the lake edge until at last it was near enough for her to climb. When she was safely in its branches, the tree moved out to the center of the lake again.

After a long search her parents came to the lakeside and saw her in the tree. They called and called, but she would not come down. At last her lover came, and it was he who persuaded her to return home and take up her pot-making again.

COMMENT

That a tree rescues the creative artist and saves her from attacks by the practical, unimaginative side of the community is significant.

The artist is given the protection of nature because the artist is in tune with nature, is part of nature. In despair because she is not understood and given credit for her creativity, she wanders in the wilderness for three days. Three is perhaps the most potent number of all: in J. C. Cooper's *Illustrated Encyclopaedia of Traditional Symbols* (p. 114), the meaning of that number is extensively discussed. "The Triad is the number of Whole, inasmuch as it contains a beginning, a middle and an end," said Aristotle. Birth, life, death; body, soul, spirit; past, present, future; father, mother, child; Father, Son, and Holy Ghost . . . "Three is the 'heavenly' number, representing the soul, as four is the body."

Wandering in the wilderness—that is, passing through periods of despair before one reaches the life-giving waters of the lake of inspiration—is a well-known phenomenon in the life of a creative artist. The artist sees the tree at the center of the lake but cannot reach it by herself. It has to come to her. She has gone as far as she can go by her own efforts, but they are not enough. The tree—the inspiring spirit, the "grace of God"—comes to her and takes her up in its branches. *Up* in its branches. How often when an artist is creating is he or she aware of help from someone or something beyond the self?

When the girl in the story reaches this point, and only then, she can return to the ordinary world—but she doesn't want to return. Her parents call her, but she refuses to return. Only her lover can call her back. Only love is an emotion strong enough to counteract fear and despair. She will return under her lover's protection. She will create her pots again, enriched and wiser from her experiences of rejection and suffering.

Source of myth
  Geoffrey Parrinder, *African Mythology.*

Invisibility

African/Nigerian

A forest spirit called Musa once spoke to a man, a hunter looking for food for his family. In the great forest full of trees, the spirit singled out twelve types of tree and told the man that if he crushed some of the bark of these twelve trees into powder and then mixed the powder with water, he would have a paste to spread on himself that would make him invisible to the animals of the forest.

COMMENT

People have always longed to be invisible—the hunter more than most, and the journalist with camera no less than the killer with arrow or gun.

In the forest full of trees the spirit singled out twelve types of tree. For anyone accustomed to dealing with symbols the number twelve in this context comes as no surprise. Twelve is a most potent number in any culture. J. C. Cooper, in *An Illustrated Encyclopaedia of Traditional Symbols* (p. 120), says that the Duodecad is a complete cycle. It represents cosmic order. "As three times four it is both the spiritual and the temporal order, the esoteric and the

exoteric. There are twelve signs of the zodiac and twelve months of the year," twelve hours of the day and night, twelve fruits of the cosmic tree, twelve members of the council of the Dalai Lama, twelve disciples of Christ, twelve tribes of Israel, twelve labors of Heracles, twelve knights of the round table, twelve gates and foundations of the holy city of the New Jerusalem, twelve in a modern jury—the list goes on and on.

One tree alone would not confer invisibility; twelve types are needed. By the time the hunter has sought out the twelve types of tree he must know a lot about the forest. By the time he has gathered the bark and ground it and made the paste he has become so knowledgeable about nature and so in tune with its ways that he no longer stands out as an alien in the forest. In a sense he has *become* the forest.

Because this is a myth and because the language is symbolic, the intent of the hunt is not only to kill an animal for food in the literal sense but to rid oneself of one's alienation from nature. We want to become "invisible" in the sense of dropping the personal identity that separates and prevents us from becoming part of the whole.

Sources of myth
Geoffrey Parrinder, *African Mythology.*
J. C. Cooper, *An Illustrated Encyclopaedia of Traditional Symbols.*

The Young Man, the Lion, and the Yellow-Flowered Zwart-Storm Tree

African

A lion found a young man sleeping by a water hole. He took hold of him and lifted him up onto the branches of a yellow-flowered zwart-storm tree. There he wedged him in between the branches while he went back to the water hole to drink. The young man woke and tried to move but found that he was held fast. The lion returned and pushed his head more firmly between the branches. Noticing that there were tears running down the cheeks of his prey, the lion licked them away and then returned to the water hole to drink, for he was very thirsty.

While he was drinking the young man managed to escape and ran away. He made sure not to run directly to his home but disguised his spoor by running first this way, then that.

When he reached his home he told everyone what had happened to him, and the whole village worked to disguise his scent by wrapping him around with hartebeest skins, for they knew it was in the nature of the lion not to let its prey go.

The lion appeared near the village. The people shot at him again and again, but he would not die. They threw children at him, but

he ignored them and would not eat. They threw women at him, but again he ignored them and would not eat. They kept shooting with arrows and with spears, but he remained unhurt. He kept sniffing for the young man. The lion wanted the young man for it had licked his tears. It wanted no one else but that young man.

The lion attacked the houses and knocked them down. The people pleaded with the mother to give him her son. At last she said she would, but insisted that the lion must die.

"Let the lion die and lie upon my son," she said.

The people gave the young man to the lion, and the lion killed the young man. The people shot at the lion once more, and the lion said, "Now I am ready to die. For I have the young man that I put in the yellow-flowered zwart-storm tree, the young man whose tears I licked, the young man that I have all this time been seeking. Now I have hold of him, for I am his."

And so the lion died and the people laid his body on the body of the young man.

COMMENT

The young man is sleeping by the water hole. That is, he is in a state of non-awareness right beside a life-giving source of spiritual nourishment.

The lion (his spiritual guide, his god, his destiny) sees him and puts him in the tree (the cosmic tree of life). He is off the ground (the mundane world) and is waiting for his entrance into the higher world—the world of the higher consciousness.

The lion delays, knowing that the young man cannot be rushed but must go through certain phases. The lion sees the first stirrings of awareness in the man. The young man's first reaction to his awakening in the tree is despair, sorrow, fear. He weeps. The lion licks away his tears. He tries to comfort him and goes away again, giving him more time to come to terms with his situation. The man does not want the fearful agony of awakening to the higher self. He runs back to his old ways, cunning enough to do everything in his power to avoid pursuit.

But he cannot escape his destiny. The lion will not take a substitute. It is that particular young man who is marked, and only he will the lion take.

In the lion's final words we find the key to the whole story.

The lion and the young man are one. The flight and the chase are within the one soul.

Have we not all feared the awakening in the yellow-flowered zwart-storm tree, knowing that our lives will never be the same again and there is no way out but complete death to the world?

Some years ago I wrote a poem about the fearsomeness of the spiritual call that has helped me to understand this story.

The Christ

He will not come
as you expect,
swinging incense
and a Bible . . .

He will come
like a tiger from a field of daisies . . .
suddenly leaping
from the familiar
to the divine.

Incidentally, I'm not at all sure what a yellow-flowered zwart-storm tree looks like or even whether it exists in Africa, but the name works very well symbolically in this story. The yellow flowers suggest the golden brilliance of light—the fertile flowering of spiritual experience. "Zwart" is the Dutch word for "black," and "zwart-storm" conjures up for me images of those fearsome black storms that terrified me when I was a child in Africa. Those storms cleared the air after days and weeks, sometimes months, of sultry brooding weather that made it hard to breathe and dried the veld so thoroughly that it appeared parched and dead, only to spring alive again as soon as the storm broke.

This tree is a combination of light and dark—of gentle flowers and fierce and driving storm.

This tree is life.

Source of myth
Alan Garner, *The Guizer: A Book of Fools,* reprinted in *Parabola* XI(4) 1986: 82–84.

The Baobab Tree

African/Hausa

There was a chief who had three sons. He decided to test them to see which son was worthy to succeed him.

Near the gate of the chief's house a huge old baobab tree grew. The father told the sons to show their skills in the exact place where the baobab was growing.

The three young men mounted their horses and considered the situation.

The eldest son came galloping up to the tree. He threw his spear at the tree, and where it passed through he followed it on his horse. He rode on.

The second son came galloping at the tree, and when he was near enough he pulled the horse up and leaped over the tree. He rode on.

The youngest son rode up to the tree. He gripped the branches and heaved and pulled until he had uprooted it. Then he rode to his father and showed him the tree in his hand.

"Now I ask you," says the storyteller, "who excelled among the chief's sons? If you do not know, that is all."

⚘ COMMENT ⚘

The baobab is an extraordinary tree. It grows very slowly and

sometimes lives for more than a thousand years. It is also called the "upside-down tree" because its twisted and wizened branches look like roots, and there are legends among the Bushmen that the trees fall, fully grown, from heaven, landing upside down. People have even claimed to hear the thud of their falling.

Three sons are being tested by a father—a very common theme in myths and legends. The story is a teaser. We are not told the father's decision and are left to struggle with the solution ourselves.

That the sons have to test themselves on the exact spot where the baobab grows is significant. This is not a test of physical skill, for the baobab is a magical tree from the otherworld, and to enter its space is to enter a realm other than the physical.

The first two sons leap through and over it and do not return to their father. The third brings the tree to the father.

Traditionally, stories of this kind involving three sons, daughters, sisters, or brothers end with the third person doing the right and noble thing and achieving what has to be achieved. If we take this as a similar case, we must assume that the father was most pleased with the third son. To us, with our present need to preserve trees at all costs for our own survival, the action of the third son is wanton vandalism, but to a primitive tribe, brute strength might well be most admirable.

If we take the story as depicting the three layers of consciousness of the one individual, which we also have been led to expect by reading countless other myths and legends, we look for the three stages of development of the chief's son. We could say that the first son leaps through the lessons of the spirit world and brings nothing back to his own life; we could say that the second son similarly leaps over and brings nothing back. The third son, however, takes the whole teaching of the spirit world and brings it back with him to use when it is his turn to lead the tribe.

Source of myth
    Harold Courlander, *A Treasury of African Folklore.*

Willow Wife

Japanese

Heitaro loved the willow tree that grew close to his hut. As the world judged riches he had none, but the tree was treasure and temple and company enough for him, and each new season of the year seemed more beautiful than the last. When the wind blew through its branches, no music was finer.

One day the villagers came with their choppers and threatened it.

"We need the wood," they said when Heitaro protested. "We are going to build a bridge."

"I will find the wood for you," he cried. "Don't touch the willow."

He scoured the land and came back to them with wood. They departed, leaving the willow unharmed.

That night as the moonlight shimmered on its leaves he stood beneath the willow branches and gave his thanks to the gods that the tree had been spared.

Something moved. A sliver of moonlight? He turned and peered into the shadows. There stood a beautiful young woman.

He bowed to her and apologized for disturbing her. He backed away, believing that she was waiting for her lover.

She watched him go.

The next night she was there again—and the next. She was indeed waiting for her lover, and Heitaro at last realized that it was he himself she came to see.

They were married and lived happily. A child was born to them, and each night they prayed in the willow temple.

But one day the emperor To-Ba ordered that a temple to Kwannon, the goddess of mercy, should be built in the district. For this temple the villagers demanded the wood of the willow tree and would not be turned aside.

Heitaro was sad, but because he now had a wife and child, he believed he could endure the loss.

The villagers began to cut the tree.

The willow wife cried out, "Husband, the room is growing dark!" She fell to the ground and covered her face with her hands. Heitaro saw her limbs twisting and turning as though to avoid blows. He found he could do nothing to help her. He and his daughter watched as the willow wife lay dying. When the last blow on the tree was struck, he was alone with his daughter.

COMMENT

I hardly like to sully this simple and exquisite tale with comment. The profound love of the man for the tree and of the tree for the man speaks for itself. The bridge is a practical earthly object, and the villagers can use other wood, but for a temple ordered by the emperor they need the best. I cannot help feeling that no temple built by man would ever be as holy as the willow tree. The goddess who lives with us in our homes is destroyed in order to build a temple in which only a statute of her is kept. The spirit of the tree is the true goddess and lives while the tree lives. Kill the tree and you kill the goddess. The temple is a poor substitute for the living goddess.

Source of myth
> Based on a Japanese folktale, retold by Iyanaga Mitsuyo, and quoted in Meinrad Craighead, *The Sign of the Tree: Meditations in Images and Words.*

The Wonderful Birch Tree

Russian

O ne day a man and a woman set out to look for a sheep that had gone astray. In the woods the woman met a witch who turned her into a black sheep and then turned herself into the likeness of the woman. The witch in the guise of the wife then called to the man to tell him that the sheep had been found.

Back in the man's home the witch suggested that they should slaughter the sheep there and then to keep it from running away again. The man agreed.

The daughter, who knew that the black sheep was really her mother, ran to her and told her what was to happen. The mother told the girl that she must be careful not to eat any of the slaughtered sheep, and that afterward she must gather up all the bones and bury them by the edge of the field in the woods.

The girl did as she was told, and from the bones of her mother a beautiful birch tree grew.

In time the witch had her own daughter by the man, and she treated the elder girl like a slave about the house.

One day there was to be a festival, and all were invited to the king's palace to celebrate. The witch-woman made sure the elder

girl was to stay home while she took the younger with her to the party. Before she left she set the girl to picking up a bowl full of barleycorns she had deliberately thrown among the cinders of the hearth.

The girl, finding that the task was impossible, sat weeping by her mother's grave. Suddenly she heard her mother's voice tenderly asking her what the matter was. She told her, and her mother suggested that she take one of the branches from the birch tree and strike the hearth with it crosswise. She did this and found to her delight that all the barleycorn flew back into the bowl. The hearth was spotlessly clean.

She took the branch back to the tree and laid it on her mother's grave. Her mother then told her to bathe on one side of the tree, dry herself on another, and dress on the third. After she had done this, the girl found herself transformed into a beautiful young woman, magnificently dressed. Her hair was partly of gold, partly of silver, and partly of something more precious still. Waiting beside her was an elegantly caparisoned horse.

She sprang on the horse and rode to the palace. There the prince took charge of her and kept her by his side at all times. The witch-woman's daughter, however, gnawed the bones under the table. Thinking she was a dog, the prince pushed her aside with his foot, and her arm was broken.

When the beautiful young woman came to leave, her ring caught on the latch of the door, for the king's son had smeared the door with tar. She had to ride off without her ring.

By the time the father, the witch, and the younger girl returned home, the elder daughter had returned her fine clothes and steed to the birch tree and was back in the kitchen. The witch-woman boasted that her daughter had been the companion of the prince and claimed that her arm had been broken in a fall.

Some time later a second festival was held, and all happened much as before. The witch left the elder daughter at home to pick up a pot full of hemp seed spilled among the ashes. A branch from the magical birch tree sent them flying back into the pot, and the older girl again went to the palace, dressed magnificently. The king's son never left her side once—but again, moving his legs while they were feasting, he broke the leg of the witch's daughter, who was under the table gnawing the bones.

When the elder daughter was ready to leave, she was so anxious to get back before the witch discovered she was not in the kitchen that the golden circlet from her hair stuck fast to the tar the prince had smeared on the doorpost.

Again the witch boasted that it was her daughter the prince had fancied.

A third festival was arranged.

This time the witch poured milk on the hearth and charged the girl with the task of getting it back into the jug as white as ever.

Again the birch branch proved to be magic, and the elder girl arrived at the palace as beautiful and as richly dressed as before.

The witch's daughter got her eye knocked out as she crouched under the table, and the elder girl lost her golden slippers as she rushed off, for the prince had smeared the threshold with tar.

Then a fourth festival was announced—this time to find the maiden whose finger fitted the ring, whose head fitted the circlet, and whose feet fitted the golden slippers.

The witch filed down her own daughter's finger, head, and feet. She saw to it that the ring, the circlet, and the shoes fitted and that the elder girl did not get a chance to try them on. The prince was forced to take the witch's daughter as bride. But while they were in her father's house, the elder daughter whispered in his ear, "Alas! dear Prince, do not rob me of my silver and my gold."

The prince instantly recognized the maiden he loved.

He set off with both girls to the palace, but when they reached the river the prince threw the witch's daughter over to serve as a bridge and left her there.

Weeping, she prayed that a golden hemlock would grow from her to show her mother where she was and what had befallen her.

Living happily in the palace with the prince, the elder daughter bore him a son. When the news of this event reached her father's house, the witch set off at once to visit the child, thinking it was her own grandson. On the way she found the bridge with the golden hemlock growing out of it. She started to cut it down to take to her grandson and heard it crying out that it was her daughter.

As soon as she heard what had happened, she transformed the plant and the bridge back into her daughter and stormed on to the palace. There she put a spell on the young princess so that she became a reindeer in the forest and substituted her own daughter in the prince's bed.

The baby cried and would not be comforted, for he could see that the woman who now held him was not his mother.

Worried about his son, the prince called a wise widow-woman to divine why the child was so unhappy. She told him at once what had happened to the child's mother. They discussed what was best to be done and agreed that the widow was to take the child to the woods the next day to give him some fresh air. There the widow called the reindeer, and each day for three days the reindeer came, took off her reindeer skin, and nursed her son.

The child was undoubtedly happier, but the king's son could not be content until he found a way to get back his wife. The widow suggested a plan of action.

The day before the reindeer herd was due to migrate to distant grazing lands, the widow told the reindeer-woman she wanted to comb her hair one last time.

So, while the reindeer-woman nursed her child, the widow-woman combed her hair, the king's son threw the reindeer skin into a fire and burned it to a cinder.

"I have nothing to cover me now, poor creature that I am," the young woman cried, and transformed herself first into a distaff, then into a wooden beetle, then into a spindle, and into all imaginable shapes. But all these shapes the king's son went on destroying until she stood before him in human form again.

Then they returned to the palace.

At sight of them the witch-woman and her daughter fled. They were never seen again.

⚚ COMMENT ⚚

There are several interesting contrasts and parallels in this story. For instance, the young daughter realizes that the witch-woman is not her real mother; her baby son recognizes that the witch-woman's daughter is not his mother. In both cases the grown-ups are taken in, but not the child. Out of the good mother grows a birch tree; out of the witch's offspring grows a hemlock. According to J. C. Cooper (*An Illustrated Encyclopaedia of Traditional Symbols*), the birch tree symbolizes "fertility; light; protects against witches and drives out evil spirits." According to Scandinavian and Teutonic lore, the "last battle in the world will be fought round a birch tree . . . The birch tree is the Cosmic Tree of shamanism, and the shaman ascends the seven or nine notches of the tree trunk or birch pole, symbolizing the ascent through the planetary spheres to the Supreme Spirit." Hemlock represents "death; deceit; ill-luck."

Another parallel is that the witch takes the place of the real wife, and the witch's daughter takes the place of the real daughter.

At the beginning the man and the woman are looking for something they have lost when the wife encounters the witch. Could it be that the something that is lost is something in their relationship? What if the wife is not replaced but is actually the same wife—her lower self, her mean, selfish side that has come to the fore so that she sets about destroying her higher self? In a sense she has put her soul in another place, leaving herself soulless. The daughter never loses faith in the good side of her mother and goes to the woods, the sacred grove where it is possible to communicate with the spiritual realms. When she acts under the instructions of her true mother and uses the magical birch branch (that is, uses the higher self), she accomplishes her tasks easily, but when she tries to do them in the ordinary way they are impossible.

The product of the happy marriage, when the wife is in her higher mode, is a beautiful, noble girl with whom the prince falls in love. The product of the unhappy marriage, when the wife is in her lower mode, is a poor child who suffers all kinds of maiming and disfigurement, lurking as she does in the darkness under the table like a beast.

Why does the prince put tar on the latch, the door, and the threshold? These are all parts of the door—the entrance to the otherworld. In a sense he is a godlike figure trying to keep her in the higher world, the world where her higher self will be at home. But she is not yet ready to stay. Each time she ventures in with the help of the good side of her mother, she leaves some part of herself behind as a kind of pledge or hostage. What does the ring represent? It could be fidelity. She pledges her loyalty to the ideal of the higher self. The circlet of gold from her head could represent her spiritual and intellectual awareness. Her golden shoes could be her connection with this earth or the means by which she moves from one realm to the other. The three symbolic objects are rich in meaning.

She returns home, where she is mistreated because she is still not capable of withstanding the evil forces represented by the witch-mother.

Only when the witch's daughter is about to usurp her place at the prince's side does she speak out at last and make a commitment: "Do not rob me of my silver and gold." She realizes what she will lose if she does not make a positive stand now. Seeing that she has recognized her true self at last, the prince takes her to the palace.

That the witch's daughter becomes a bridge is significant. It is over the bridge of the tests and trials the elder girl has been submitted to that she is now capable of entering the palace and being accepted as belonging there. She would not have even discovered that the birch tree on her mother's grave was magical if she had not been in trouble and seeking help. The tree represents the deeply rooted part of her mother—the eternal part that is still alive and growing beyond this world. Praying to her for help, the girl receives help. The hardships inflicted on her by the witch and her daughter are the bridge over which she eventually passes to the palace.

But even when the golden girl has everything she wanted—the prince and her baby son—she is still vulnerable to attack by evil forces. She must undergo more trials before she will be strong enough to really take charge of her higher self.

She nurses her baby but is not capable of breaking the spell by herself. Even when her husband and the wise widow do it for her, she is in a panic because she is naked. She cannot grasp that what she is is enough to please God. She tries to hide behind various guises, most of which are connected with housewifery and ordinary worldly matters. It is as though she is saying, "I am only a housewife. How can I be expected to reach the mystical heights of self-realization that you expect?"

Only when the prince has destroyed every false guise and she has nowhere to hide is she strong enough to face the antagonist.

The witch at this point recognizes that she no longer has power over her and flees.

The similarities with the Cinderella story are obvious. Meinrad Craighead, in *The Sign of the Tree* (p. 144), describes a version of the Cinderella story very reminiscent of the Russian tale. She points out that it is an "ancient and universal custom to plant a tree over a grave in the belief that it will give strength to the soul of the dead person" and, by the power of its symbol as ancient as that of Osiris in Egypt, draw the buried seed of the soul up into the air and sunlight where we can communicate with it. Cinderella's father gave her a hazel twig, which she planted on her mother's grave. When the tree grew, a white bird made its nest in the branches. "To Cinderella's surprise, whatever she secretly longed for the bird brought to her. When Cinderella hugged the hazel tree she knew her mother's body again and when the bird flew to her with gifts she knew it was her mother's hovering spirit."

To emphasize again the way in which myths express universal human experience in symbolic form, how many of us have noticed that when someone very close to us has died, it seems for a time as though everything we do is watched and everything we need is provided? The sense of a "presence" in spirit form helping us is very strong and very comforting, but in spite of this, we long to take the person in our arms again. Perhaps we too should plant a special tree for them so that we will have some physical form to hug in their name. In fact, we often do. My family planted a flowering cherry in my garden on the day of my husband's funeral. Churchyards are full of trees planted as memorials to the departed.

The natives of Amboina, in Indonesia, used to plant clove trees to mark the birth of each child. The Rev. Hilderic Friend mentions this custom in his book *Flowers and Flower Lore* and believes the rebellion of 1775 was due to the Dutch cutting down these birth trees to keep the price of cloves up.

Today, even in the materialistic West, we often plant trees to mark notable events. While such a tree lasts we believe that somehow the memory and the influence of that event is kept alive.

Source of myth
Andrew Lang, *The Red Fairy Book*.

Yggdrasil, the World Tree

Scandinavian

In the apparent emptiness of chaos, before anything was manifest, coldness existed and heat existed. These two collided in the emptiness, and from their mingling the process of manifestation began. First there was Ymir and then there was Bor, the father of Odin. Ymir was destroyed by his own offspring and became the earth, the sea, and the sky. Halfway between frost and fire the realm of Midgard came into existence.

Asgard was established as the region for the gods, where Odin, the all-father, dwelled, and the twelve Aesirs.

Yggdrasil, the mighty ash tree, grew at the center of all, rooted in all the realms from the darkest to the lightest, from the lowest to the highest. Each day the gods met in council beneath its spreading and shady branches, reaching it only by crossing a burning rainbow bridge guarded by a fierce being.

In the first ages it flourished and bloomed, and all about it was beautiful and pure. But at one point the gods began to fear the cold that had not mingled with the heat to create being. They began to fear the icy breath that threatened to unbalance the conditions on which existence relied, and they asked Loki to build a fortification around Asgard to keep the frost out. He employed a builder, who demanded that the price for his work would be the

sun, the moon, and the goddess Freya. The Aesirs agreed, but when the wall was nearly finished they realized that they did not want to pay the price, and Loki tricked the builder out of his fee. Thus, with the breaking of an oath, evil entered the nine realms, and Yggdrasil was beset by enemies. An immortal goat and four stags fed on its buds and bark, worms gnawed at its roots, and a serpent-dragon made its nest beneath it. Iduna, who had granted apples of immortal youth, fell from her home in the boughs to the dark depths beneath.

At the top of the tree an eagle still sat, with a hawk perched on his forehead, but now he was in perpetual conflict with the serpent at the root. A mischievous squirrel ran up and down the tree, carrying insults and threats from one to the other.

The tree would have perished if the three Fates who sat at the foot of it had not watered it daily from the well of life, on which swam two swans. The nine branches, or worlds, were continually renewed as they were destroyed, and Mimir, the god of memory and wisdom and knowledge, took up his abode among the leaves, drinking daily from the pure spring of wisdom that rose from beneath the tree.

When the Fates sang of ceaseless but harmonious change, the leaves of the great tree rustled, and the eagle that sat on its topmost bough flapped his wings in delight. Even the serpent at the root forgot to gnaw.

At one time Odin hung in agony from the tree for nine days and nine nights, with his side pierced and bleeding, until he at last gained the knowledge of the spirit runes he was seeking—the knowledge that would give him power over all things. A draft from Mimir's spring, paid for by the removal of one of his eyes, ensured that he would remember what he had learned.

In the latter days of the first age, when there was a great battle between all the forces of good and all the forces of evil, the tree shook and swayed. It moaned and cried like a living being as the gods were destroyed one by one. But it withstood all turmoil until at last it succumbed to an all-consuming fire and the old order was gone forever.

From where they were hidden deep within its roots, a man and a woman crept out, blinking at the new bright world that was growing from the tree's ashes.

COMMENT

The Norse held out against the Christianization of Europe longer than most, many of them setting sail in their longboats to avoid the hated change that was engulfing their neighbors. So it was in far-away Iceland that the rich fund of stories handed down orally for centuries was preserved in their pure form much later than in the rest of Europe. They were finally written down as poems, the *Edda*, by a Christian priest, Sigmund Sigfusson (Saemund the Wise, 1056–1133), and as prose a century later by Snorri Sturluson (1179–1241).

The stories are complex, often contradictory and confusing, as all great mythological teachings are after passing through the minds of generations of storytellers, but certain broad patterns emerge that are universal.

There is chaos, out of which order emerges. There is a time when life-forms come into being, proliferate, and are named. There is a period of consolidation when the created order is respected. There is a moment when a crucial failure to obey the unwritten law that keeps the whole in harmony starts the long fall back toward chaos. The gods struggle among themselves, polarizing into good and evil forces, light and dark, until finally the disparity is so great that the inevitable tremendous confrontation and conflict lead to the destruction of all that has been so painfully and slowly built up. The worlds have returned to silence and lifelessness. But, like a green shoot emerging from a bare field, a man and a woman emerge—a new Adam and a new Eve, a new heaven and a new earth. A new cycle begins from the charred remains of the old.

At the center of all this stands the great ash tree, Yggdrasil, a fitting symbol for stability, growth, and regeneration. In this tree the action of the universe is played out. Manly P. Hall says of the tree: "The single source of life and the endless diversity of its expression has a perfect analogy in the structure of the tree. The trunk represents the single origin of all diversity; the roots, deeply imbedded in the dark earth, are symbolic of divine nutriment; and its multiplicity of branches spreading from the central trunk represent the infinity of universal effects dependent upon a single cause. . . . The growth of the universe from its primitive seed may be likened to the growth of the mighty oak from the tiny acorn. While the tree is apparently much greater than its own source, nevertheless that source contains potentially every branch, twig, and leaf which will later be objectively unfolded by the processes of growth" (*The Secret Teachings of All Ages*, p. xciv).

At the crown of Yggdrasil, on the very topmost bough, sits an eagle with a hawk on its head. This is often identified with Odin, the all-father, himself. At the crown of the kabbalistic tree of life is the deity called I AM THAT I AM—the highest name we know for *that which we cannot know*. The eagle and the hawk are both birds that fly high and see far. That one can give a lift to the other, so that its range is magnificently extended, is significant for us. Every attempt of the god in the macrocosm mirrors our own attempts in the microcosm to identify with our higher selves. "As above, so below," as Hermes Trismegistus in the Emerald Tablets declared.

In some versions of the myth there is an even greater eagle flying out of sight above the tree. Again we are reminded of the sefirotic tree of the kabbalists. Above all the realms—above all the names of God—is another higher, ineffable, inexpressible, unimaginable, nameless ONE.

The serpent that lies at the root may represent the dark powers at the root of our subconscious, which lie in wait and are always at war with our higher selves. Manly Hall says, rather, that the serpent so often shown around the roots or the trunk of the tree "usually signifies the *mind*—the power of thought—and is the eternal tempter or urge which leads all rational creatures to the ultimate discovery of reality and thus overthrows the rule of the gods" (*The Secret Teachings of All Ages*, p. xciv).

At any rate, the squirrel that runs up and down is an inspired symbol for that busy, chattering, restless part of our mind—for that troublesome, doubting dialogue that goes on continually within us and often holds us back from fulfilling our true spiritual potential.

There are two springs at the foot of Yggdrasil: one life-giving, one wisdom-giving. We are reminded of the two trees of Eden: one life-giving, one knowledge-giving.

The three Fates water Yggdrasil with the waters of life. The balance must be meticulously kept between the worms, the stags, and the goat trying to destroy the tree, and the waters of life renewing it daily. Without the balance between life and death, cold and heat, light and dark, the dynamic of existence is destroyed.

The gods failed to honor their promise to the builder of the wall because they realized if they had gone ahead they would have destroyed the balance between light and dark. Indeed, they ordered it to be built in the first place because they feared the effect of too much "cold."

Many events happen in the tree. Iduna dispenses golden apples of immortal youth. Mimir, representing wisdom and memory, lives. Odin takes on the sacrificial role of his own cult and hangs for nine days and nine nights (remember the nine worlds or realms contained in the tree), bleeding from a spear wound in his side, until at last he gains the revelation he seeks by such suffering: the secret, spiritual meaning of the runes.

Lately, in what has come to be known as the Aquarian Age, there has been a great revival of rune lore, and many rune sets and rune books present various divination methods. I would always advise people to go very carefully with any divination method and not lose their grip on their traditional faith or their sense of everyday reality.

But nevertheless remarkable results can sometimes be obtained. I once asked a psychic friend to cast the runes for me in the hope of obtaining a message from my husband, who had recently died. This was the result: "Failure to face up to death consciously would constitute a loss of opportunity. Give up gladly the old, and be prepared to live for a time empty. Develop inner stability. Do not be seduced by the momentum of old ways while waiting for the new to become illuminated in its proper time" (Ralph Blum, *The Book of Runes*). The message could not have been more apt.

To return to Yggdrasil, we are warned that in the end even the tree cannot stand against the fires of a holocaust unleashed by the war of the gods, but though everything we have ever known is destroyed, the potential for life is still there and we are given another chance. Many religious myths have a similar great cyclical pattern, for example, the vast cycles of the Hindu myths. Even our spiral galaxy turns slowly through the ages like a great wheel.

Our greatest fear is that we may fall back into the void and cease to exist. Our myths must give us hope.

> *The sun turns black, earth sinks in the sea,*
> *The hot stars down from heaven are whirled;*

Fierce flows the steam and the life-feeding flame,
Till fire leaps high above heaven itself.
But then, behold!
Now do I see the earth anew
Rise all green from the waves again:
The cataracts fall, and the eagle flies,
And fish he catches beneath the cliffs.

> From the Eddas, quoted by Joseph Campbell in
> The Masks of God: Occidental Mythology, *p. 486.*

Sources of myth

H. R. Ellis Davidson, *Scandinavian Mythology.*
Alexander S. Murray, *Manual of Mythology.*
M. W. Macdowall, *Asgard of the Gods: The Tales and Traditions of Our Northern Ancestors.*
Joseph Campbell, *The Masks of God: Occidental Mythology.*
Manly P. Hall, *The Secret Teachings of All Ages.*
Ralph Blum, *The Book of Runes.*
Michael Howard, *The Wisdom of the Runes.*

The Orange Grove and the Enchanted Canary

Flemish

Prince Désiré found that he could not love any of the young women who were presented to him at court. "They are too pale, father," he said. "They do not interest me." Then one day the prior of the Abbey of Saint Armand presented him with a basket of oranges, a fruit little known at that time in northern Europe, with a note saying that they had come from a land where the sun always shone.

The prince decided he would go on a journey to that land and there seek a bride.

After a long journey he came to a land where the sun was warm, and he believed he was nearing his destination. His horse stopped without any command at the edge of a forest, facing a little hut, on the doorstep of which sat an old man. They greeted each other, and the man prepared a meal for the youth.

"May I ask you where you are going?" the old man said.

The prince told him he had had a dream that in a sunny land there was a grove full of orange trees and that in one of those oranges he would find the woman who was to be his wife.

The old man smiled and wished the young man well. "Go, young man, follow your dream, and if you do not find the happi-

ness that you seek, at any rate you will have had the happiness of seeking it."

The next day, when it was time to go, the old man gave the prince advice.

"The grove you seek is not far from here," he said. "In the depths of the forest you will come to a park surrounded by high walls that cannot be scaled. Behind the walls is a castle in which a horrible witch lives who allows no one to enter. Behind the castle is the orange grove. There is a gate in the high wall, but the hinges are so rusty it will not open. Oil the hinges, and the gate will open by itself. Once through the gate you will be threatened by a huge and vicious dog. Throw him an oatcake. Next you will see a fiery oven with a giantess attending it. Give her this brush. Last, you will find a well on your left. The cord is moldy, so take it and spread it in the sun. Don't attempt to enter the castle, but walk round it and go into the orange grove. There pick three oranges and leave as quickly as you can. Once out of the gate, leave the forest by the opposite side." Then he added a stern warning. "Whatever happens, do not open your oranges till you reach a riverbank or a fountain. Out of each orange will come a princess, and you can make your choice. Once having chosen, be careful never to leave her for an instant. Remember that the danger that is most to be feared is never the danger we are most afraid of."

Désiré found that everything transpired as he had been told. But just as he was about to return to the gate, the sky darkened and a terrible voice called for his destruction. But the giantess refused to throw him in the oven because he had given her a brush to scour the oven more easily, the dog refused to bite him because he had fed him, and the rope refused to strangle him because he had spread it in the sun to dry. Even the gate refused to fall on him because it had been oiled.

The young prince rode swiftly away from the place. The way was long and he grew very thirsty. He decided to eat one of the oranges, but instead of juice the fruit contained a canary, which flew out at once and asked for a drink. He slit open the second and a second canary appeared. Both birds flew away in search of water.

Then Désiré realized he had not obeyed the instructions of the old man. He dared not open the third orange until he came to a river or a fountain.

Eventually he came to a river and opened the third orange. To his disappointment a third canary flew out. "I am thirsty!" she cried. He lifted water from the river in his hand and let her drink. As soon as she had drunk, the enchantment was lifted and she became a beautiful princess.

When they were near his father's castle, Désiré told the princess to wait in the forest by a pool until he could prepare a proper welcome for her. He rode on to tell his father and all the court about the beautiful wife he was bringing to be his bride.

Meanwhile an ugly, lazy, and bad-tempered girl went to the pool to draw water. Afraid of the stranger, the princess hid in a willow tree, but as she peeped out her reflection fell on the still surface of the pond. The other girl thought it was her own reflection and at first believed it was she who was so beautiful. When a movement from the princess revealed her mistake, the girl was furious and determined to make her suffer for the mistake she herself had made. She enticed the shy princess down from the willow tree, and on hearing that she was to be the prince's bride, she offered to dress her hair so that she would look prettier at the wedding. The innocent princess was grateful, but the not-so-innocent girl made sure she drove a pin into her head. As soon as she felt the pin, the princess turned back into a bird and flew away.

Then the ugly, lazy, bad-tempered girl passed herself off as the prince's bride. She assured him when he looked doubtful that as soon as she was wed she would become beautiful once again. Having dispelled one enchantment, the prince felt confident he could dispel another, but the people were dismayed to see how ugly and unpleasant the prince's bride looked.

When all the guests were gathered for the wedding feast, a canary appeared in the kitchen and sang so sweetly that one by one the cooks and scullions were beguiled into letting the food spoil and burn.

The king and the prince stormed into the kitchen to find out what was amiss. The pin in the head of the bird was noticed and removed, and the canary became the beautiful princess again—just in time.

⁓ COMMENT ⁓

The orange is a fruit of the sun—of light. The prince apparently had everything he could wish for, but he was restless and dissatisfied. He set off on a quest, ostensibly to find a wife but actually to find his higher self. A wise man, a sage, gave him guidance, and all went well when he obeyed. Before he could reach the orange grove there were many dangers to overcome and several acts of kindness to perform.

He obtained the magical oranges and was well on the way to the spiritual state of bliss he was seeking when he made his first mistake. Physical discomfort (thirst) made him forget the instructions and open the oranges before he reached water. That is, he thought it wouldn't do any harm to relax the discipline a little. Just in time to prevent the loss of all he had gained, he remembered what he was supposed to do. No matter how hungry and thirsty he might become, no matter how much he felt like despairing, he must keep the treasure safe until the right time and place—until a source of spiritual sustenance was present to revive and renew him. The bird became a princess, and he set off for home, having achieved the means of his transformation—but not quite. Again, complacency made him forget the sage's instructions. He left the princess alone while he went to boast about what he had achieved. That was his second mistake. Many dangers beset the search for the higher self, and what is gained with difficulty can be lost with ease. The prince was duped and was unable to distinguish between true spiritual magic and chicanery.

Luckily, the princess herself took the initiative, and grace saved the day.

Source of myth
  Andrew Lang, *The Red Fairy Book.*

The Twelve Dancing Princesses

French

There was once a little herd-boy whose name was Michael but who was always called "star-gazer" because he was always dreaming.

One hot summer's day he went to sleep under an oak and dreamed he was visited by a beautiful lady, dressed in gold, who told him to go to a certain castle where he would find a princess to marry.

The next day at the same hour he went to sleep again under the same tree, and the same dream occurred.

When the dream came a third time he decided to go off and find the castle and the princess he had been told about.

As he approached the castle he was told that there were twelve princesses living in the castle. Very proud and spoiled they were, enjoying great luxury. But strangely, although they were locked in their bedroom every night, their satin shoes were found dusty and scuffed and worn every morning. When asked what they had been doing all night to wear out their shoes, they always replied that they had been sound asleep.

This was such a mystery that the king announced he would allow anyone who could solve it to take his pick of the princesses to marry. Many fine princes came and watched at the door of the

princesses' bedchamber all night, but in the morning the princes had disappeared and the shoes were worn through as before.

When Michael, the star-gazer, arrived at the castle, he took a job assisting the gardener. One of his first tasks was to present each princess with a bouquet of flowers in the morning. Eleven of them took the flowers haughtily with never a glance at him, but he met the eyes of the youngest, Princess Lina.

That night the lady in the golden dress appeared to the star-gazer once more. This time she was holding two young laurel trees, a golden rake, a golden bucket, and a silken towel. She told him to plant the two laurels in two large pots and take great care of them, raking them with the rake, watering them with the bucket, and wiping them with the towel. When they were grown to the height of a girl of fifteen he could ask them for anything he wished.

When he woke he found the two laurel trees beside him. He planted them and took great care of them as the lady had charged him, and when they were grown he asked one of them to make him invisible. Instantly a white flower appeared on the tree and he put it in his buttonhole.

That night he followed the princesses to their bedchamber and watched as they dressed themselves in their most magnificent ball gowns instead of their nightclothes. Then they put on their satin shoes and opened a trapdoor in the floor.

The star-gazer followed them as they descended a flight of steps. So eager was he to keep up with them that he trod on the skirt of Princess Lina. For a moment he thought she had noticed him, invisible though he was. But when she complained, her sisters assured her that no one was there.

At the bottom of the steps was a passage. At the end of the passage, a door. Through the door the princesses trooped. They walked quickly through a wood that shone like silver, then through a wood that gleamed like gold, and finally through a wood where the leaves glittered with diamonds.

Then they came to a lake, on the shore of which were twelve little boats, each containing a prince eagerly grasping the oars. Each princess stepped into a boat, and Michael, the star-gazer, stepped into the one with the youngest princess. Because of his extra weight the boat went through the water more slowly than the others.

At last they disembarked and entered a castle, where in a magnificent ballroom the princesses and their partners danced all night.

Michael wished that he too could be a handsome prince dancing with the princesses, but he did not realize the princes were all under a spell, having been given a philter by the princesses that froze their hearts and left nothing but the love of dancing.

At first cock-crow the ball was over, and the princesses hurried back to their home. In the last wood Michael broke off a silver twig, almost alerting Princess Lina to his presence. Her sisters assured her that the sound she heard was nothing more than an owl hooting in the turret.

Michael managed to get back to the garden safely.

That day he put the silver branch among the flowers he presented to the youngest princess. She said nothing, but that night while dancing she looked everywhere for the young gardener without seeing him.

On the way back through the golden wood one of the older princesses thought she heard the crack of a twig, but this time Lina assured her it was nothing more than the screech of an owl in the turret.

The next morning when she found the golden twig in her bouquet she called the young gardener to her and offered him a bag of gold to keep his silence about their secret. The boy refused the gold but said that he had no intention of telling the king.

For the next two nights Princess Lina noticed nothing untoward during their secret trip, but on the third she heard the diamond twig snap.

Her sisters, noticing that she talked to the garden boy and looked at him more than she should, teased her for being so interested in a commoner. At last she told them that the boy knew their secret but had told no one, not even the king who would have rewarded him with one of them in marriage. They wanted to throw him in the dungeon at once, but the youngest refused to allow it, so it was agreed that he would be invited to the ball and there given the philter that would render him harmless.

Michael heard their plot and went to the second laurel tree and asked to be dressed like a prince. A pink flower appeared, which he placed in his lapel, and at once he was dressed like a prince. He obtained permission from the king to watch the door of the princesses' bedroom in an attempt to solve the mystery of the worn shoes.

He was taken openly to the secret castle this time, and there he danced with each of the princesses in turn. The youngest found that he was the best partner she had ever had, but she spoke to him haughtily, suggesting that he had fulfilled all his ambitions now that he was being treated like a prince.

"Don't be afraid," he replied. "You shall never be a gardener's wife."

A feast was served and a large golden cup was brought in.

"The enchanted castle has no more secrets for you," the eldest princess said. "Let us drink to your triumph." And she passed the cup first to the star-gazer.

Michael looked longingly at the youngest princess for a moment and then lifted the cup to his lips, although he knew very well what it would do to him.

"Don't drink!" cried Princess Lina. "I would rather marry a gardener!"

Michael flung the cup to the ground and the contents spilled out. At once the spell was broken. The other princes became normal men again.

On hearing the story the king made the young gardener a prince, and he and the youngest princess were married. But when she heard how he had managed to fool them, she cut down the laurel trees so that he would never again have such an advantage over her.

⚘ COMMENT ⚘

Because there are twelve princesses and the secret activity that is such a mystery occurs at night, and because it is a golden lady that comes to the herd-boy in his dreams, we cannot help assuming that the story is a sun myth. In very ancient times the sun was always seen as a female goddess; only more recently did it become known as the sun god. Hence, we assume it is a very old story indeed, though no doubt it has been altered over the centuries so that the golden lady can be associated with an angel rather than with the sun itself.

The activities of the twelve princesses (the twelve daytime hours) are open for all to see in the day—but when the sun goes down, who knows what the twelve hours of the night are up to? As a sun myth the story shows some parallels with the ancient Egyptian sun myth. At night the hours cross a lake by boat—the solar boat that glides so silently across the heavens.

The potent and meaningful dream comes to the herd-boy under an oak tree, thereby reinforcing the expectation we have that trees are points of contact with the otherworld. Our association with trees as magical living beings closely bound up with the mystical life of the spirit is further emphasized by the fact that there are two wish-granting laurel trees. That the laurel trees have to be carefully cultivated in a particular way underlines our need to exert ourselves if we want to be in a position to have our wishes granted.

The princesses and the boy pass through three woods. Again, trees and sacred groves are mysterious, mystical places that we have to pass through before we reach the otherworld—the place of deeper or higher consciousness. Each wood is progressively more precious and rarefied than the last: silver, gold, diamond.

The sun goddess desires to release the princes, the hours of the night, and the princesses, the hours of the day, from the spell that dooms them to perpetual motion without love. She chooses as her instrument a herd-boy—an honorable, natural boy, unspoiled by society and still capable of visionary and mystical experiences. He is capable of love.

The princesses, no less than the princes, do not know how to love. They are haughty, proud, and spoiled. They move about in the perpetual cycle of day and night, night and day, but without love the whole thing is meaningless.

The youngest, least conditioned by her upbringing, begins to notice something unusual about the nightly routine and to feel the first stirrings of emotion, but even when she learns about Michael and understands that he will not betray them she is so used to the class prejudice and false values of her upbringing that she cannot bring herself to give herself to him rather than to the emasculated princes. Only when he is about to sacrifice himself to be with her on the only terms she will allow does she realize what he means to her. She understands that marrying a gardener who loves her is better than dancing a million nights with an elegant prince who does not and cannot love. True, heartfelt love has broken the spell, and the golden lady must have been happy to see the cosmos infused at last with the most beautiful and powerful of forces. We remember the first few verses of I Corinthians, chapter 13: "Though I speak with the tongues of men and of angels, and have not charity, I am becoming as sounding brass, or a tinkling cymbal. And though I have the gift of prophecy, and understand all mysteries, and all knowledge; and though I have all faith, so that I could remove mountains, and have not charity, I am nothing." This is from the King James version; the Revised Standard Version gives the word "charity" as "love." No word catches exactly what is meant here. "Charity" has become associated with dropping coins into collecting boxes, and "love" with rolling about naked on a bed. Why is there not a perfect, unsullied word that describes this pure and beautiful emotion—the love that surpasses understanding?

It is often said that we should not put our own contemporary interpretations on ancient myths. If this is a myth about the sun goddess and the hours of the day and night we should read it only as such. For a scholar this may be enough, but for me the whole value of myths, their secret and undeniable power, is that they *can* be interpreted by each culture, each generation, in ways that are meaningful to that particular culture or generation. The way in which a myth differs from an ordinary story is exactly the way in which it describes something that pertains to all of us irrespective of time and place: the inner, universal, eternal journey of our souls. Similarly I have often been told that because certain things in the Bible have their roots in older cultures (the hero floating anonymously on the river and being found by a princess to grow up as the savior of his people, the king sacrificed for the people, the forbidden tree) the Bible therefore does not record "truth." But to me, as to many others, the very fact that in so many cultures and so many times the same themes and the same meaningful incidents are reported reinforces my belief that the Bible *is* "telling the truth"—universal, eternal, mythic truth that is greater than factual truth and makes of factual truth something greater than it is. If the Bible were only mundane fact telling us that so-and-so lived in such a year, in such a place (though this is of course significant), its power to resonate with our experience of life would long since have ceased. The mythic, symbolic content of its story gives it the power to make us shiver and gasp and *know* that it is true.

Similarly, an ancient story about the hours of the day and night gains significance for us only when we are touched by its mythic, symbolic relevance to our own situation.

Source of myth
Andrew Lang, *The Red Fairy Book.*

Merlin and the Hawthorn Tree

British

When Merlin was an old, old man (and none could give a count of all his years), a young girl came to King Arthur's court. Some said she was the handmaiden of the goddess who had emerged from the lake to give the sword Excalibur to Arthur. To look upon she was beautiful beyond belief, but none could see into her heart.

Her name was Vivien, and she watched the wonders of the court closely, soon becoming envious of Merlin's great powers. She determined to learn all she could from him and so beguiled him with her flattery and her beauty that he, sighing, followed her wherever she went and easily gave her secrets that were best kept hidden.

But Vivien was not satisfied with what she learned. She claimed that Merlin was teaching her no more than a child could learn. She wanted more and deeper mysteries to be revealed to her. He demurred, saying that she was not ready. Then, afraid he would not be able to withstand her pleas and knowing that some mysteries were too dangerous and powerful to be entrusted to someone so young and unwise, he left the court and went across the sea to the forest of Broceliande in Brittany.

She followed him, weeping and telling him her heart was broken because he did not trust her.

At last, with a cunning alternation of the granting and the withholding of sexual favors, she wheedled out of him his last and most closely kept secret: how it was possible to imprison a man within a tree. Within seconds of obtaining knowledge of this spell she implemented it. The mighty Merlin, the wisest of all men, was confined forever within a cage of bark—a hawthorn tree.

COMMENT

Merlin, or Myrddin, is one of the great figures of British legend. Bard, prophet, necromancer, spiritual guide, and sage, he predates the story of King Arthur, yet most people know of him only in association with that "once and future king."

In the *Dictionary of Non-Classical Mythology* he is listed thus: "Merlin/Myrddin was god of the British or Brythonic Celts, whose personality in later medieval legend, like that of Arthur, generated into a mere wizard or necromancer. He is the folklore representative of a great deity. He may be identical with the sun-god Nudd. Professor Rhys puts forward the suggestion that he may have been the deity specially worshipped at Stonehenge, the erection of which tradition refers to him."

Bob Stewart, in an article in *Legendary Britain,* expresses doubt that Merlin ever became "a besotted old fool" tricked by an "alluring young girl." He believes that this is a later and unscrupulous inversion of the truth and that Merlin derived his power in the first place "from the influence of, or under the guidance of a feminine archetype, goddess or power." It is more than probable that Merlin, the wild man of the forest and the great revelatory force of nature, knowing that all things have their time and place and realizing that he had served his purpose and should step aside for a new age, voluntarily passed on his magical lore to one chosen by the goddess, a young and vigorous woman, and willingly allowed himself to merge back into nature—the hawthorn tree (which even today is associated with the magic and mystery of the pre-Christian religion). In Tennyson's poem "Vivien," the girl imprisons him in an oak, a tree deeply associated with the ancient druidic religion.

Another powerful event associating the Merlin story with trees occurred in his youth. After witnessing the horrors of battle, he is said to have fled to the great forests of Scotland, torn off his clothes, and endured for many years a kind of holy madness in which he lived like the animals. From this period in his life came inspired prophecy and deep, enduring wisdom. At this stage he lived with the trees and drew strength and wisdom from them. Later he reached a stage when he became one with them—he became tree—and freed thus from having to express himself in words that could be so easily misunderstood and distorted, he communicated as trees communicate: wordlessly, but profoundly. It may be that he is still communicating with those who are sensitive enough to understand what he has to say. Lady Charlotte Guest tells us of at least one occasion when he managed to make himself heard. Sir Gawain, suffering a temporary enchantment as a dwarf, received comfort and advice from Merlin, who appeared as fine smoke surrounding the tree in which he was imprisoned in the forest of Broceliande (*The Mabinogion*, p. 384, quoting from Robert Southey's preface to *Morte D'Arthur*).

On the other hand, several scholars posit that the name "Merlin" does not belong to one man alone but is a title, like "High Priest" or "King," won and held throughout the ages by different individuals, highly trained and developed. Imprisonment in the tree marked symbolically the end of the ancient pagan religion brought about by the Christian church, often referred to as female, "the bride of Christ."

It is significant that Merlin did not die. He was imprisoned and there thus remains always a possibility that one day he will be freed and will return.

In many minds Vivien became associated with the dark female force—the destructive aspect of the goddess and the necessary but nevertheless uncomfortable counterpart to creation.

Sources of myth

Michael Senior, *Myths of Britain*.

Alfred, Lord Tennyson, "Vivien" in *Poetical Works of Alfred, Lord Tennyson*.

Marian Edwards and Lewis Spence, *A Dictionary of Non-Classical Mythology*.

Bob Stewart and John Matthews, *Legendary Britain*.

H. A. Gueber, *Myths and Legends of the Middle Ages*.

Lady Charlotte Guest, *The Mabinogion*.

The Glastonbury Thorn

British

T he old man was weary. It seemed to him they had been travelling forever.

First there was the pain of seeing his nephew crucified—the one good man who could have led them away from the violence and greed, the endless jockeying for power, the exploitation, the fear, and the terrible yoke of the Romans. He had always loved him, long before they knew who he really was. He was Mary and Joseph's little boy, bright-eyed and eager to learn everything there was to learn, full of unexpectedly wise sayings, always giving the impression of great strength and at the same time great gentleness.

In those early years he had never really believed Mary's claims for him; indeed, he had worried that the child's head would be turned by all the adulation he was receiving from friends and relatives. On several occasions he had taken the boy with him on his expeditions just to get him away from the people who hung on his every word. He felt the boy was growing intellectually too fast for his own good. Even the rabbi came to the house to debate with him, and the neighbors gathered outside the doors and windows to listen, astonished at his learning and murmuring their praise—sometimes even shouting it aloud. He spent too much time

with scholars and old men. Joseph of Arimathea was himself an educated man and valued learning—but a child must have a healthy body, not just a well-developed brain.

Mary hated to see her child go on these expeditions, but she knew that it would be good for him and he would be safe with his uncle—as safe as he could ever be in this unsafe world. She often feared her son would say something to a Roman soldier that would draw attention to himself. She had not forgotten that desperate journey to Egypt to escape Herod's murderous rage at the prophecy that a child born at the same time as her son would become king of the Jews. She had hated being away from her home for so many years among strangers and strange customs.

She and her husband had kept the Jewish traditions in their little home, but outside their four walls the child had been exposed to other ways and other beliefs, even as a toddler. At four and five he had spoken with Egyptian priests, questioning them and learning from them. Joseph remembered how worried she'd been when they returned to Nazareth that her son's questing mind, and the eagerness with which he searched out beyond his people and his people's religion, would divert him from the great purpose for which he had been born.

Joseph of Arimathea was a merchant and had travelled the world often accompanied by his nephew, meeting with silk merchants from China on the high plateaus beyond the Caspian Sea, Indian merchants from the steamy lowlands, Arabians from the desert, Africans from Ethiopia. He had even been to this remote island in the western ocean off the coast of Gaul to load his ships with tin and lead. Everywhere they went the boy watched and listened and observed. Everywhere they went he asked questions.

Who would have thought, the old man mused, it would end like this. He had looked forward to a comfortable old age among his own people. Already during his last few journeys as a merchant he had realized that he, who had always loved travel, was tired of travelling. Now there was no hearth of his own waiting for him. He was an exile—a man on the run.

He remembered that terrible, terrible day that was as dark as night, that moment when he looked up at the young man on the cross and knew for the first time that Mary had been right about him—he *was* the Son of God, he *was* the Messiah they had been waiting for all those centuries—and realized that he had never fully appreciated who his travelling companion was. What a waste! What questions he could have asked! Too late! Too late! He had always been so busy: battling with the sea, bargaining with the locals, loading the ships. He had been so keen for the boy to learn the practical skills that would fit him for life on this earth, forgetting that it was foretold he would have very little time on this earth and in that little time he had to turn it around from spiritual darkness to light.

During the last few years before the crucifixion he had not seen his nephew much, but he had heard a lot about him and was proud of what he was doing. But he had not really paid much attention. Busy. Busy. Getting and spending. Getting and spending. Well, at least his wealth had given him status in the community— a status he had put to good use when he persuaded the Romans to allow him to bury his nephew in his own tomb instead of leaving him out on the hillside to have his bones picked by kites like any common criminal.

He had not seen the risen Christ, but he believed the reports of Mary and the disciples who had seen him.

In the years that followed, after he was driven from his homeland with others who had been close to the Christ and were now regarded by the authorities as dangerous dissidents, after the long and hazardous sea journey to Gaul and the long land journey seeking a place to call their own, he had had time to think back to when his nephew had been his companion. He remembered things that now left him no doubt that his nephew was who he said he was. How blind he had been—how stupid. He had thought all along that he was the one in charge—the leader, the teacher. Never once had he noticed that everything that happened when Jesus was with him was very different from what happened to him when he was on his own. He had seen things, heard things, understood things in a way he never had before. He had thought it was coincidence that when the boy was with him many more people gathered around them. He had scarcely noticed that sick people got better at his touch, that bitter and angry people began to smile and sad people to forget their sorrows. He had been with the Son of God and he had shouted at him for letting a rope slip or for dropping a bale of wool! If only he could make that time return.

Well, he could not. But he'd make sure others did not make the same mistake. He would draw out of his memory every word the Savior had spoken and every word that his followers remembered he had spoken. He would teach what he had been too preoccupied to mark at the time. But there was too much for him to remember. If only . . . if only . . .

In Gaul the little group of fugitives had wandered from place to place, talking, preaching, and founding communities of Christians. One by one they had parted and gone their separate ways. Joseph himself had spent a long time with Philip, the apostle, who had established a mission among the Gauls. There he had learned a great deal about the druids, the Celtic priesthood. At last, because he had had some experience of Britain and some smattering of the language of the natives, Philip had suggested that he should go to that country and establish a bridgehead for the Christ there, taking with him eleven companions.

When they had landed, some of them had wanted to set up their community right there, but Joseph had felt the place was not right. He could not explain it; he just knew it was not the right place. And so they had set off, by small dinghy and by foot, carrying all they could manage, Joseph himself leaning more and more heavily on a stick, feeling his age. Time and again they stopped, and time and again he persuaded them to go on. He did not know what he was seeking, but he knew he would know it when he found it.

At last they came to a place—a hilly island rising from the surrounding marshes like a beacon, green and forested, an island that was sacred to the druids, who believed it was the entrance to the otherworld where the dead went to await rebirth.

"This is the place," said Joseph of Arimathea, and he plunged his staff into the rich, soft soil.

His weary companies unloaded their packs and sank down thankfully. They had wondered whether he would ever stop.

The sun was already sinking, staining the far western sea and the waters that lay around them blood red. Some felt a chill of uneasiness. This place had a power they did not understand. Others felt relieved and happy, as though they had come home.

They made camp where they had stopped, prayed, and settled down for the night.

In the morning the staff that Joseph had placed in the earth was rooted and flowering.

"This is the place," he said again, this time with satisfaction. He had known he would be given a sign—and here was the sign.

The little community did not have an easy time of it at first. They had chosen to establish their mission at the heart of the ancient religion they were trying to displace, and the opposition was great. But at last, after long and tactful negotiations with the local ruler and strenuous debate with the druid priests, Joseph managed to win twelve hides of land* on which to farm and live. That both druids and Christians believed in an afterlife and that the Deity was "Three in One" helped to ease the way. The miracle of the flowering staff was accepted at once and understood.

For a while the Christians were busy establishing themselves on the land and attending to the everyday business of survival. At last they were ready to build a chapel of wattle-wood and thatch and to start their ministry.

From a nearby well sacred to the ancient earth goddess, Joseph drew water in the chalice he had brought from Jerusalem—the chalice from which the Christ had drunk at his last meal on earth, the chalice they had raised to catch his blood as he hung on the cross.

With this water, poured from this chalice, he purified the land where they were to build their church, and he baptized his first converts.

The church itself he dedicated to Mary, the mother of the Savior, for it was built on the site of a temple to the triple goddess of the Celts in her three aspects of young virgin, mother, and wise woman. Before the coming of the Celts, he was told, this same place had been the site of an even older goddess. Mary would incorporate all that these ancient female forces had stood for in the hearts of the people and would lead them further to a new age.

---

*In present terms, approximately 1,440 acres.

On the rough stone altar of this early church, Joseph laid a cross fashioned from a branch of his flowering thorn tree—for it was the miracle of this tree that brought most of his Celtic converts to him.

⚘ COMMENT ⚘

That Joseph of Arimathea, supposed to be the uncle of Jesus of Nazareth, came to Glastonbury in Somerset and founded the first Christian church in Britain is a most persistent legend. It is not as far-fetched as it may at first sound. Trade between Britain and the Mediterranean countries and the Middle East did take place in ancient times. Cornish tin was much sought after for Bronze Age weapons, and merchants would go to great lengths to obtain it. Once familiar with the tin-mining areas, curious travellers might well go further inland to see what else they could find to trade. The great Severn estuary and the rivers, such as the Parrett, that flowed into it could convey boats deep into Somerset. Langport was a handy river port well known to the Romans.

Bishop Godwin de Prae Sulibus, writing about A.D. 1600, claimed that there was an ancient manuscript in the Vatican referring to the expulsion of Joseph of Arimathea, Lazarus, Martha, Mary Magdalene, and others after the death of Stephen. They were put into a ship and sent off at the mercy of the sea, eventually landing at Marseilles. The story is taken up by the Roman Bishop Treculphus, who said that Philip, the evangelist, preached in Gaul "and having much to do with the Druids there who passed between Gaul and Britain, sent twelve missionaries, whereof Joseph of Arimathea was one, who came to Glastonbury A.D. 63." Both these pieces of information are found in a most interesting book published in 1909: *Chapters on the Early History of Glastonbury Abbey*.

When Saint Augustine was sent to Britain by Pope Gregory the Great in A.D. 596, he found an already well-established Celtic church claiming foundation by God himself just after the death of Christ.

The first royal charter given to Glastonbury (then called Inys Witrin) by Rex Dumnoniæ in 601 refers to an old church already there. But it was only in later times, when the Benedictines arrived, that Glastonbury became such a rich and mighty center of learning and Christianity, boasting a great library and many precious relics.

Glastonbury has always been a place of pilgrimage, from very ancient pagan times, when it was thought to be the entrance to the otherworld guarded by the fearsome Gwyn ap Nudd, through the Christian era and still today, though its monastery and abbey were shamefully ruined by Henry VIII when he dissolved the monasteries in England and vandalized the sacred buildings.

The three thorn trees in Glastonbury are said to be the descendants of Joseph's original staff: one in the grounds of St. John's Church in the High Street, one in the garden of the abbey, and a windswept wisp of one on the bare slopes of Wearyall Hill. This holy thorn is reputed to flower at Christmas and Easter, and the tradition is that a sprig of it is sent to the reigning monarch every year. It is not a hawthorn native to England but a type of hawthorn well known in the Middle East. Hawthorn was a tree very sacred to the ancient Celts, and the fact it was a hawthorn that burst into blossom must surely have influenced the Celtic acceptance of the miracle.

The flowering of an ordinary stick as proof of a message from the Divine is not uncommon in religious myth and legend.

A prime example was Aaron's rod in the Old Testament (Numbers 17:2-5, 7, 8). After there had been a great deal of controversy as to who should be high priest, the Lord spoke to Moses:

> Speak unto the children of Israel, and take of every one of them a rod according to the house of their fathers, of all their princes according to the house of their fathers twelve rods: write thou every man's name upon his rod. And thou shalt write Aaron's name upon the rod of Levi: for one rod shall be for the head of the house of their fathers. And thou shalt lay them up in the tabernacle of the congregation before the testimony, where I will meet with you. And it shall come to pass, that the man's rod, whom I shall choose, shall blossom: and I will make to cease from me the murmurings of the children of Israel, whereby they murmur against you. . . .
>
> And Moses laid up the rods before the Lord in the tabernacle of witness.
>
> And it came to pass, that on the morrow Moses went into the tabernacle of witness; and behold, the rod of Aaron for the house of Levi was budded, and brought forth buds, and bloomed blossoms, and yielded almonds.

After that there could be no argument. Aaron had been chosen by the Lord.

Ovid's *Metamorphoses* tells of another leadership contest settled by a flowering branch. Romulus threw his spear. It stuck fast in the Palatine hillside and "suddenly put forth leaves," grew roots, and became a shady tree. Rome was founded on that place.

It is said that Saint Christopher set out to find the most powerful prince on earth, was baptized by a hermit, and was given the task of carrying travellers over a river. One of the travellers he carried was Christ—more powerful than the most powerful prince on earth. As Christopher set him down on the ground his staff began to flower like a palm tree. In Christian iconography Christopher is usually depicted wading through a river with a living tree in his hand, carrying the Savior on his shoulders.

In the early years of the Celtic church in Britain, wandering Irish monks set off in little boats of hide and wicker and landed on the coasts of Wales, Cornwall, Devon, and Somerset like so many floating seeds. When they landed, often after a long time on a stormy sea, they set off on foot, seeking the place that the Lord had appointed for them and expecting to know it by a sign. Saint Patrick told Saint Benignus, "Set out on your journey and when you come to the place the Lord shall show you, plant your staff and see how it will grow." Saint Benignus followed his instructions and by this method discovered the place to found his monastery at Ferremere.

The Cornish or Breton Saint Melor was murdered on the instructions of his uncle. The assassin cut off his head, stuck it on a staff of wood, and set off to show it to his employer. On the way the assassin became ill and cried out for help. The head spoke and told him to plant the staff in the ground. He did so. The staff took root and grew immediately into a tree bearing healing fruit, and a fountain of pure water sprang up at its root (William Anderson, *Green Man*, Chapter 3).

Later, in Anglo-Saxon times, the same sign was accepted. On her journey from Northumbria to the island of Ely, Etheldreda, an Anglo-Saxon saint of the seventh century, found that wherever she spent some time resting, her staff bloomed. Around each of these trees a little community of Christians gathered and chapels were built.

Of course, Saint Patrick's instructions might have had a completely practical application as well. Where a cutting takes root easily, the soil is sure to be rich and fertile and thus a good place to live and grow food.

An interesting aspect of the Glastonbury thorn legend is that one of the relics listed in old records of the abbey was Aaron's rod. There is nothing like a biblical authority to give power to a symbol!

The miraculous flowering of the bough out of season must surely be a reference to the power of God, the creative force, over the laws of nature. Even today, in an era of extraordinarily advanced high technology, we cannot control nature, though we have found to our cost that by breaking its laws consistently we can effect changes that cause a dislocation of the natural order. We have the power to change certain things, but because we do not know the whole picture and dynamics of interrelationships, we get one thing under control only to find another going disastrously wrong.

But God, the legends of the flowering boughs imply, can do anything he wishes. He can make a dry stick bloom suddenly out of season, and nothing else will be adversely affected. That is one reason for using this particular image to make a point about God. But there are other reasons for its effectiveness as a mythic image.

It draws on ancient religion for its impact. To the earliest people, nature *was* the deity. They did not envisage a separate being "out there." The goddess was the earth itself—mysterious, powerful, her own mistress. They were at her mercy. They could accept her gifts for their use but could make no changes in her immutable laws. Only she could change them if she had a whim to do so; that is why so much time and effort was spent in trying to placate her. The Greek myth of Demeter and Persephone shows her power. When Demeter was mourning for her daughter, the world became a dark and icy place all year around, but when Persephone was returned to her, albeit for only six months at a time, apparently dead sticks budded and blossomed.

An image, particularly one that is understood the world over because it is based on worldwide common experience, is more effectively used in a new religion if it draws on the suggestive power of the religion it is displacing. The masculine Jewish God, outside nature, gains credibility in this instance by performing deeds that had been regarded as exclusively the preserve of the earth goddess within nature.

Another idea is suggested by these flowering bough stories. In the Bible we are told that God fashioned man in his own image. Persistently, artists take this as a license to depict Jehovah as an old man with a beard sitting on a chair in the sky—an image difficult for a thinking person to accept.

However, something in the human being, which cannot be depicted by the artist or described in words, *does* partake of the nature of God, though in a form that is no more than a faint reflection of a reflection of a reflection to the power of infinity. We call it consciousness, but it is not the type of consciousness dependent on the physical body. It is another deeper kind of consciousness that many of us have experienced even though it has not been scientifically proved. It can be called "soul-consciousness," and it may be this consciousness that can make boughs blossom. When Aaron's rod and Joseph's and Etheldreda's staffs bloom, the message is that they are men and women so in tune with God that they are capable of using that force within them that was made in God's image. They are therefore men and women who can be trusted to bring us safely nearer to a relationship with the creative divinity.

The power of soul-consciousness in us to make boughs blossom reminds me of an experiment conducted a few years ago with a well-known British healer. He has proved time and again that his great capacity to heal is based on actually being able to make changes in physical matter by no more than the power of his concentration. In one experiment, seeds were placed in three pots. One lot he ignored. The second he positively directed to grow. The third lot he directed negative energy against, visualizing them not growing at all, but withering and dying. At the end of the experiment the seeds he had done nothing about had grown normally, at the rate expected. The ones he had directed negative energy against had hardly grown at all. But the ones he had directed positive energy toward were taller and healthier than anyone could have believed possible during the time allowed.

Was it not God who made the boughs flower but the human

beings themselves—Aaron and Moses, Joseph of Arimathea, Etheldreda of Ely? Yes and no. Their attunement with God through the conscious use of their deepest and most profound faculties of soul is what may have caused the boughs to flower, creating an outward and visible sign that they were ready, and could be trusted, to deliver the message as accurately as it is possible for any human being to do so. It could have been God and humanity working together that caused the miracles.

Sources of myth

The Rev. William H. P. Greswell, *Chapters on the Early History of Glastonbury Abbey.*

Frances Howard-Gordon, *Glastonbury Maker of Myths.*

Shirley Toulson, *The Winter Solstice.*

Lionel Smithett Lewis, *St. Joseph of Arimathea at Glastonbury.*

Lionel Smithett Lewis, *Glastonbury, Her Saints* A.D. 37–1539.

William Anderson, *Green Man: The Archetype of Our Oneness with the Earth.*

Ovid, *Metamorphoses.*

Deirdre and the Yew Tree

Celtic

At the birth of Deirdre, daughter of the bard Phelim, a druid foretold that the girl would grow to be so beautiful that wars would be fought over her and many would die because of her.

Some who heard this prophecy warned that she would be put to death there and then before she could bring about these horrors, but Conor MacNessa, king of Ulster, said that he would marry her and keep her safely hidden from the world. He set her aside under the care of Lavercham, his old nurse, and visited her from time to time to see the first part of the prophecy, at least, fulfilled. Deirdre was indeed stunningly beautiful.

When she was almost old enough to wed, she told her nurse how much she pined for a younger man, and Lavercham became the link between Naoise, one of the three handsome sons of Usna, and Deirdre, the betrothed of the king. Their love grew strong and reckless, and eventually they fled to Scotland, protected by the two brothers of Naoise. There they lived peacefully for some years.

But King Conor did not give up his desire for Deirdre, and by subterfuge and treachery he enticed them back to Ireland. War and

bloodshed ensued, and the three fine sons of Usna were killed, leaving Deirdre at the mercy of Conor. For a year and a day she lived with him, but in that time she never spoke or smiled.

In the end she committed suicide, and from her grave grew a yew tree. "The branches twined and spread across the wide countryside until they found the branches of another yew which had grown from the grave of Naoise" (Frank Delaney, *The Celts*, p. 157).

⚘ COMMENT ⚘

The yew in Celtic lore is associated with rebirth, "since the yew tree, like the human spirit cannot be given an accurate age. The yew grows its branches down to the earth where they form new trunks, the old centre of the tree rots and fresh seeds grow again from within the soft centre. . . . The yew is the fountain head of youth in age and of age in youth, the new year that is born from the old, the new soul sprung from ancient roots in a seemingly fresh new body" (Colin and Liz Murray, *The Celtic Tree Oracle*, p. 62).

The Bretons believe that each corpse in the graveyard has a root of the yew tree growing in its mouth. The soul spirit of the Celt is transmigrated into the next life in a remarkable way that parallels the life cycle of the yew tree itself (Colin Murray, *New Celtic Review*, No. 34).

According to Kaledon Naddair, "the Irish Keltic Yew Divinity, Fer h-I, 'Man of the Yew,' was associated with the Druidical power to render 'invisible'" (*Keltic Folk and Faerie Tales*, p. 77).

Is it the darkness—the sense of hidden and secret space under a very old yew—that suggested this power to the ancients?

I cannot help thinking of William Wordsworth's magnificent poem "Yew-Trees":

> *Huge trunks! and each particular trunk a growth*
> *Of intertwisted fibres serpentine*
> *Up-coiling, and inveterately convolved;*
> *Nor uninformed with Phantasy, and looks*
> *That threaten the profane;—a pillared shade,*
> *Upon whose grassless floor of red-brown hue,*
> *By sheddings from the pinning umbrage tinged*
> *Perennially—beneath whose sable roof*

Of boughs as if for festal purpose decked
With unrejoicing berries—ghostly Shapes
May meet at noontide; Fear and trembling Hope,
Silence and Foresight; Death the Skeleton
And time the Shadow;—there to celebrate,
As in a natural temple scattered o'er
With altars undisturbed of mossy stone,
United worship; or in mute repose
To lie, and listen to the mountain flood
Murmuring from Glaramara's inmost caves.

Sources of myth

Frank Delaney, *The Celts.*
Colin Murray, *New Celtic Review*, No. 34.
Colin and Liz Murray, *The Celtic Tree Oracle.*
Kaledon Naddair, *Keltic Folk and Faerie Tales.*

The Piqui Tree

South American Waura

The blue cotinga bird chief had two wives, and they were very happy. Then one day he took two more.

These two he took with him each day to the garden where he grew the gourds, leaving the first two behind. His first two wives grew jealous. This was the first time jealousy had been known to the tribe.

"Let us take a lover," one said to the other.

"Let us, indeed," agreed the other.

So they walked through the forest to the river, whistling boldly and provocatively and carrying leaf parcels of delicious food. They were accompanied by a little owl, their friend.

On the riverbank they called and called, "Alligator-spirit, come and have sex with us!"

For a while nothing happened. Then the river churned and boiled, the earth rumbled, and the air trembled. Yakakuma, the monstrous alligator, was coming out of the water toward them.

The young women clung together in fear but did not run away.

When Yakakuma was on the bank beside them, his alligator skin slipped off like a discarded garment and he stood before them as a handsome and magnificent young man. From his ears hung earrings of feathers.

The young women gave him their gifts of food, which he took eagerly and ate with relish. Then he lay down on the ground and invited them one by one to straddle him.

Slowly they drew off their belts and gave them to the owl to keep.

They made love, and each time after the excitement the Alligator-spirit-man fainted. The women cradled him in their arms and sang him back to consciousness.

At evening, when the white mist was rising from the river, the Alligator-spirit put on the garment of his alligator skin again and slipped back into the water. The air trembled, the earth rumbled, and the water churned and boiled.

When he was gone the two young women returned home through the forest, arriving before their husband returned from the garden where he had been with his other two wives.

Many times this happened, and the husband suspected nothing. But one day the women in the garden told him that a worthless paca was eating their gourds, so the man lay in wait all one night with his bow drawn, ready to kill the paca.

At dawn, through the cold mist, he saw the creature eating his plants. He stalked closer, his arrow well aimed.

But suddenly the paca called out, "Don't shoot me, grandchild! There is something you should know. Come with me and I will show you that your wives make love to an animal while you are away from them."

The man was astonished and followed the creature to the riverbank, where they both hid and watched.

Sure enough, the two women appeared. They called and whistled for the Alligator-spirit, and the man saw that the water churned and boiled, the earth rumbled, and the air trembled. A monstrous alligator came to the bank beside the women, divested himself of his skin, and as a beautiful young man pleasured the women all day long.

The man drew his bow and in his anger was about to shoot the alligator.

"No! No!" cried the paca. "You cannot kill him by yourself. You must have all the men of the tribe to help you."

So the man went home after he had seen the alligator returning to the water—the air trembling, the earth rumbling, the water churning and boiling.

He lay in his hammock and the two wives tried to climb in with him, but he pushed them away. He was jealous of the Alligator-spirit.

In the men's house he told the others what he had seen. The men told the women that they were going on a special fishing expedition far away. When they were all gone in their long canoes, the women went down to the water's edge and eagerly called their lover.

The men hiding in the forest saw the water churning and boiling, the earth rumbling, and the air trembling. The men saw the great Alligator-spirit revealed in all his magnificent manhood before the women. The men saw the excitement of the women. They drew their bows and killed the Alligator-spirit. They flogged his skin and dragged it through the grass and over the rocks. They beat the wives and killed the little owl who held their belts. And when they had made a great fire to burn all that was left of the Alligator-spirit and his skin, they returned triumphantly to the village.

The two women stayed to mourn their lover and watch and weep by the funeral pyre. They saw that a mighty tree, the piqui tree, rose from his burning chest. When the fire had died down they picked the fruit of the tree and found that it was as sweet and as juicy as sex with their lover.

Many times the women went to the tree and ate of its fruit. They invented the bull-roarer so that they could frighten the men away from the tree and keep its secret for themselves.

But one day the men took the bull-roarers away from them, and to this day the women of the Waura tribe are not allowed to wield the bull-roarer.

But they still eat the fruit of the piqui tree.

COMMENT

The erect phallic tree gives its fruit secretly to the women when the men have done everything in their power to limit and control the sexual drive and satisfaction of the women. The tree is often the symbol of fertility and sexual gratification. Did not Adam and Eve "know" each other carnally after eating the fruit of a forbidden tree in Eden?

And what of the little owl that watched and looked after the belts of the women and is killed by the men when the lover is killed? We remember that Bloddued, the faithless wife in the Welsh Mabinogion story is punished by being turned into an owl. The symbolism of the owl seems to swing between "wisdom" and "darkness and death." Here she symbolizes "carnal knowledge." the wisdom of sex. That she hunts at night associates her with secrecy, darkness, something hidden and frightening. Something that pounces on its prey—just as the sexual drive does.

The bull-roarers must have been regarded by the men as extremely insulting and provocative. They are the women's revenge—a way of mocking the men's genital equipment. No wonder the women are no longer allowed to wield them.

From the worthless little paca, who to save its own skin "tells tales" on others, to the saga of sex, jealousy, and revenge, this story is basically the same story the world over. At the center of it is the Tree—the symbol of the natural fertile force of the earth, the life-giving force that cannot be destroyed or ignored no matter how hard we try.

Source of myth

> This story was told during the BBC 2 television program *Bookmark*, March 7, 1990. The storyteller was Aruta of the Waura tribe of the Matto Grosso, central Brazil. Program producer, Jean-Paul Davidson.

The Sacred Cottonwood Tree and the Sun Dance

North American Sioux

One of the most important rites of the Sioux was the Sun Dance, whose details were given to Kablaya in a vision. He was told that his people were losing their strength because they had drifted away from the sacred rites. In order to get back their power, they should perform the Sun Dance, meticulously following the instructions in the vision.

Kablaya instructed the people that to perform the Sun Dance correctly they must prepare themselves for four days. "This dance will be the offering of our bodies and our souls to the Great Spirit," he said. He advised them to make a large drum of buffalo hide and said he would teach them the sacred songs that must be sung. "The drum," he reminded them, "is round because it represents the universe, and the beat represents the living heart at the center of the universe."

"In this new rite which I have just received," he said, "one of the standing peoples has been chosen to be at our center; he is the rustling tree, or cottonwood; he will be our center and also the people, for the tree represents the way of the people. Does it not stretch from the earth here to heaven there? And when we pray do we not raise our hand to the heavens, and afterwards we touch

the earth, for is our spirit not from the Great Spirit and our bodies from the earth?"

Then Kablaya instructed his people in all the songs, the dances, and the signs and symbols that should be used in the ceremony. The most important of all was the finding and setting up of the sacred tree.

Scouts were sent out to seek the sacred rustling tree and were instructed that when they found it they must mark it with sage. Then they returned to camp, where they were questioned four times as to how they found the tree and where it was. When the elders were satisfied, the people formed a war party to go out and take the tree and bring it back to camp. They surrounded it, and Kablaya pointed his pipe toward the tree and spoke:

"Of all the many standing people, you, O rustling cottonwood have been chosen in a sacred manner; you are about to go to the center of the people's sacred hoop, and there you will represent the people and will help us fulfill the will of the Great Spirit."

Kablaya then offered his pipe to heaven and earth and touched the tree on the west, north, east, and south sides.

The chiefs and elders danced around the tree and then chose one man, of his brave and good character, to have the honor of administering the first cut. Three other men were also chosen. Each motioned with his axe three times to the tree, singing of his personal exploits and why he had been chosen for this honor. On the fourth motion the axe connected with the tree.

When the tree was nearly ready to fall, the chiefs chose a person with a quiet and holy nature to give the last blow to the tree. "Great care was taken that the tree did not touch the ground when it fell, and no one was permitted to step over it."

Six men carried it to the camp, stopping four times, and gave their triumphant war cries as they entered the sacred space where the sweat lodge for the sacred rite was to be constructed. Purification rites had already taken place, and everything was prepared for the tree, which was to be the central column of the circular lodge around which the whole ceremony would take place.

Many careful rites were followed before the sacred tree was at last lowered into the hole prepared for it. Smoke from sweet grass purified everything to be used in the final ceremony. Sacred pipes were smoked. Prayers to the Great Spirit wafted upward. "O You, Grandmother Earth, who lie outstretched, supporting all things! Upon You a two-legged is standing, offering a pipe to The Great Spirit."

"O Great Spirit," Kablaya prayed as he held his pipe up with one hand, "behold this holy tree person who will soon be placed in this hole. He will stand with the sacred pipe. I touch him with the sacred red earth paint from our Grandmother and also with the fat from the four-legged buffalo. By touching this tree person with the red-earth, we remember that the generations of all that move come from our Mother the Earth. With your help, O tree, I shall soon offer my body and soul to the Great Spirit, and in me I offer all my people and all the generations to come."

Small symbolic offerings were tied on the tree, and then it was raised up and lowered into the hole prepared. "Now all the people—the two-leggeds, four-leggeds, and the wingeds of the air— were rejoicing, for they would all flourish under the protection of the tree. It helps us all to walk the sacred path; we can lean upon it, and it will guide us and give us strength."

Once the tree was up, the circular lodge was constructed around it, each of the twenty-eight uprights that formed the circumference having a special symbolic significance.

"When all the preparations were finished, the dancers stood at the foot of the tree, at the west, and, gazing up at the top of the tree they raised their right hands and blew upon the eagle-bone whistles."

Kablaya prayed, "O Grandfather, Wakan-Tanka, bend down and look upon me as I raise my hand to You. You see here the faces of my people. You see the four Powers of the universe, and You have now seen us at each of the four directions. You have beheld the sacred place and the sacred center which we have fixed, and where we shall suffer. I offer all my suffering to You in behalf of the people."

At each of the four directions, the dancers chosen to offer the sacrifice chanted prayers. Then wooden pegs were driven into their flesh and attached to buffalo hide thongs that were attached to the sacred tree.

The men danced and danced until the pegs were torn from their bodies and parts of their flesh lay at the foot of the sacred tree. Thus they showed that the prayers they prayed for the good of the people were no idle prayers.

"I shall attach my body to the thongs of the Great Spirit which come down to earth—this shall be my offering."

~ COMMENT ~

Black Elk himself, during the telling of the story of how the Sun Dance rite came to the Sioux people, explains some important aspects of the symbolism.

"The circle helps us to remember the Great Spirit, who, like the circle, has no end. There is much power in the circle. . . . In setting up the Sun Dance lodge, we are really making the universe in likeness . . . each of the posts around the lodge represents some particular object of creation, and the one tree at the center, upon which the twenty-eight poles rest, is THE GREAT SPIRIT, who is the center of everything. Everything comes from Him and sooner or later everything returns to Him."

The thongs tied to the body of the man and the tree represent rays of light from the Great Spirit. "Thus, when we tear ourselves away from the thongs, it is as if the Spirit were liberated from our dark bodies."

The cottonwood tree was chosen for this important role for many reasons. The Sioux believe it was this tree-person who taught them how to make their tipis because the leaf is in the shape of a tipi. Old men watching children at play saw them making houses with these leaves, "for the hearts of little children are pure, and, therefore, the Great Spirit may show to them many things which older people miss."

Another reason for the choice of the cottonwood is that when an upper limb is cut crosswise, "there you will see in the grain a perfect five pointed star, which represents the presence of the Great Spirit." The people had also noticed that the cottonwood tree whispers its prayers to the Great Spirit continually, even in the lightest breeze.

Joseph Epes Brown adds his own note to Black Elk's story, pointing out that in the *Atharva Ved Samhita* of the Hindu scriptures, we find a description of the significance of the World Tree, which is quite identical to the symbolism of the tree for the Lakota: "The World Tree in which the trunk which is also the sun pillar, sacrificial post, and *axis mundi*, rising from the altar at the naval of the earth, penetrates the world door and branches out above the roof of the world" (*The Sacred Pipe*, p. 69).

This same symbol of tree as the axis mundi occurs in almost every sacred myth of the world.

Kablaya receives the rite in a vision. He must have balked at first at the thought of his flesh being torn out as sacrifice, but he never questioned the authenticity of the revelation. He knew that a people who have lost the ability to pray—that is, to communicate directly with the Great Spirit that infuses all realms and all things—is a lost people, a people using so little of their potential they might as well be blind, deaf, and crippled.

Since time immemorial, I believe, there have been waves of revelation from the Great Spirit, which have at first been believed and acted on with enthusiasm and integrity, but which, with the passage of time, have become distorted or forgotten through laziness and cupidity. Then it is time for another revelation, another renewal, another regeneration.

Kablaya knew the importance of renewal and knew that to make an impression it should not be easy. The detailed use of symbolic paint, feathers, smoke, dance, and song—too complex to have been brought into my brief summary of Black Elk's account—prepared the way for the most sacred moment of all. It is like walking the maze at the entrance to a church: we have to leave the mundane world and enter a psychological condition in which the supernatural seems more real than the natural. If we just went out into the wood and chopped down any old tree, the column we raised would be any old column. The finding of the tree, the chopping of it, the raising of it—every detail must have its ritual and symbolic significance in order to prepare the minds and hearts and souls of the people for the drama that is to occur in a realm other than the mundane. The tree itself sacrifices itself to the task. The people address it as a person, explaining the purpose for which it is required. To the Native American, and indeed to anyone with a sense that the mundane is not all we have, everything in the universe has consciousness, has soul, has the dignity of union with the Great Spirit.

The tree stands tall in its role of mediator between heaven and earth, as representative of something greater than itself calling forth from us something greater than ourselves. It and we are to become the channel of the renewal and regeneration of the sacred.

Source of myth

Joseph Epes Brown, ed., *The Sacred Pipe: Black Elk's Account of the Seven Rites of the Oglala Sioux.*

The Origin of Stories

At the end of this book I place a story about the origin of stories.

North American Seneca

Once upon a time an orphan boy, called by his foster mother Poyeshao, was sent out to hunt birds for food. Each day his foster mother gave him cracked corn to eat, and each day he came back with birds. Gradually he brought more and more birds as he became skilled as a hunter.

On the tenth day he went deeper into the forest than ever before and sat down upon a flat-topped stone in a clearing to eat his corn and mend a broken arrow. Suddenly a voice said, "Shall I tell you a story?" He looked around, startled, but could see no one. The voice promised him stories in exchange for the birds he had shot.

"What does it mean to tell stories?" the boy asked—for stories had not yet been invented.

The voice, which came out of the stone he was sitting on, started to tell a story about the ancient days and what had happened to his ancestors. The boy listened intently. At the end the stone promised more stories if the boy would bring an offering of more birds the following day.

Each day the boy hunted, gave the stone some birds, and listened to the stories. Each night he took back only part of his

catch. His foster mother was puzzled and sent another boy to watch him and tell her what he did all day that he brought home so few birds. The boy followed Poyeshao and discovered the talking stone in the forest. He too gave an offering of birds and listened to the stories.

Neither boy told the woman what was happening, and she remained puzzled that they returned so late and so tired and yet had so little meat to show for it.

After a few days more the foster mother hired two men to follow the boys, and they in their turn discovered the storytelling stone. This time, at the end of the day, the stone told them to bring the whole village the following day to listen to the stories.

The villagers came and laid offerings of meat or bread on the stone, and the stone told them stories.

"Some of you will remember every word that I say," the stone said. "Some will remember a part of the words, and some will forget them all, but each man must do the best he can. Hereafter you must tell these stories to one another."

COMMENT

This is one of the stories collected by Jeremiah Curtin from the Seneca people, published in *Seneca Indian Myths* in 1922, and subsequently quoted in full by Abraham Chapman. J. N. B. Hewitt remarks in his introduction to the collection by Curtin that some of his happiest memories were of spending time with Mr. Curtin "in discussing the larger significance and the deeper implications which are found in the intelligent study and interpretation of legends, epics and myths—the highest type of poetic and creative composition."

Abraham Chapman points out in his commentary on this story of the origin of stories that the name Seneca means "Place of the Stone" and that "rocks and stone in human antiquity were the prime medium on which events of historical importance were recorded, first in rock paintings and later in rock inscriptions and writing." He also reminds us that to Native Americans, "man is not a hierarchical super-creature but a part of the entire order of nature."

Peter Berresford Ellis, writing about the ancient Celts of Britain and Europe and their attitude to nature, could also have been describing the Native American attitude to nature.

The Celts believed "in the consciousness of all things. Trees, fountains, rivers, even the weapons and implements they used were considered to be possessed of an indwelling spirit. Everything was but a fragment of one cosmic world. . . . In *Timaeus,* Plato developed a similar doctrine of a world soul in which all matter was interrelated. This concept is remarkably illustrated in the poem of the druid Amergin recorded in the Book of Invasions. Amergin subsumes all things into his own being with a philosophical outlook that is paralleled in the Hindu Bhagavad-gita" [and, I would add, in ancient Egyptian and Native American philosophy].

> *I am the wind which breathes upon the sea.*
> *I am the wave of the ocean.*
> *I am the murmur of the billows . . .*
> —*from Peter Berresford Ellis,* Celtic Inheritance, *p. 12*

In looking closely at the little story of the origin of stories we notice several things. The boy is an orphan. He is cut off from his roots. He is sent to hunt food for the table but finds instead food for the soul. He must give offerings of birds to the storytelling stone. Birds frequently symbolize the flight of the soul—the higher self. The boy has to lay his higher self on the stone in exchange for the precious gift of the story. Flesh has to become other than flesh. It has to be offered in sacrifice.

Notice that the stone is in a forest and the boy must penetrate deeper into the forest than he ever has before. The forest is the unknown—the rich, fertile, deep forest of the living truth.

The stories he receives are of the ancient times and of his ancestors. He is given his roots that he may grow strong and tall.

At first the stories are secret. They are immensely important and must first be learned "in the heart," secretly. When the time is right they may be given to others, but even then some will remember all the stories, some will remember only a few, and some will remember none at all. That is the way of it. We suspect that the boy who listened so intently at the very beginning will be one of those who remember every word.

Story is our way of learning.

Story waits for us in the depths of the forest and teaches us about ourselves.

Source of myth
   Abraham Chapman, ed., *Literature of the American Indians.*

Selected Bibliography

Anderson, William. *Green Man: The Archetype of Our Oneness with the Earth.* London and San Francisco: Harper Collins, 1990.

The Arabian Nights. New York: Grosset & Dunlap, 1946.

Ayyap, A. S. P. *Famous Tales of Ind.* Madras: V. Ramaswamy Sastruku & Sons, 1954.

Baines, John, and Jaromír Málek. *Atlas of Ancient Egypt.* Oxford: Phaidon, 1980.

The Bible, King James version.

Blum, Ralph. *The Book of Runes.* New York: Oracle Books, 1982.

Bord, Janet. *Mazes and Labyrinths of the World.* London: Latimer New Dimensions, 1976.

Brown, Joseph Epes, ed. *The Sacred Pipe: Black Elk's Account of the Seven Rites of the Oglala Sioux.* Norman, Okla.: University of Oklahoma Press, 1953; Baltmore: Penguin, 1971.

Budge, E. A. Wallis. *Gods of the Egyptians.* New York: Dover, 1969.

Caldecott, Moyra. *Crystal Legends.* Wellingborough, U.K.: Aquarian, 1990.

———. *Daughter of Amun.* London: Arrow, 1989.

———. *The Green Lady and the King of Shadows.* Glastonbury, U.K.: Gothic Image, 1989.

———. *The Tower and the Emerald.* London: Arrow, 1985.

———. *The Winged Man.* London: Headline, 1993.

Campbell, Joseph. *The Masks of God: Occidental Mythology.* New York: Viking Press, 1959; Harmondsworth, U.K.: Penguin, 1964.

———. *The Mythic Image.* Bollingen Series. Princeton, N.J.: Princeton University Press, 1974.

Chapman, Abraham, ed. *Literature of the American Indians.* New York: New American Library, 1975.

Cook, Roger. *The Tree of Life.* London: Thames & Hudson, 1974.

Cooper, J. C. *An Illustrated Encyclopaedia of Traditional Symbols.* London: Thames & Hudson, 1978.

Courlander, Harold. *A Treasury of African Folklore.* New York: Crown, 1975.

Craighead, Meinrad. *The Sign of the Tree: Meditations in Images and Words.* London: Mitchell Beazley, 1979.

Davidson, H. R. Ellis. *Scandinavian Mythol-*

ogy. London: Paul Hamlyn, 1969, 1982.

Delaney, Frank. *The Celts*. London: Book Club Associates, 1986.

Dowman, Keith. *Masters of Enchantment*. Rochester, Vt.: Inner Traditions International, 1989.

Edwards, Marian, and Lewis Spence. *A Dictionary of Non-Classical Mythology*. London: Everyman, Dent & Son; New York: Dutton, n.d.

Eliade, Mircea. *Shamanism*. Translated by W. R. Trask. Bollingen Series. Princeton, N.J.: Princeton University Press, 1964.

Ellis, Peter Berresford. *Celtic Inheritance*. London: Muller, 1985.

Frazer, J. G. *The Golden Bough*. First published 1922. London and New York: Macmillan, 1974.

Friend, Rev. Hilderic. *Flowers and Flower Lore*. London: Rider, 1980.

Gantz, Jeffrey. *Early Irish Myths and Sagas*. Harmondsworth, U.K.: Penguin, 1981.

——, ed. and trans. *The Mabinogion*. Harmondsworth, U.K.: Penguin, 1976, 1978.

Garner, Alan. *The Guizer: A Book of Fools*. London: Hamish Hamilton, 1975.

Graves, Robert. *The Greek Myths*. Harmondsworth, U.K.: Penguin, 1955.

——. *The White Goddess*. London: Faber, 1961.

Green, Roger Lancelyn. *Tales of Ancient Egypt*. Harmondsworth, U.K.: Puffin, 1967, 1987.

Greswell, Rev. William H. P. *Chapters on the Early History of Glastonbury Abbey*. Barnicott & Pearce, U.K.: The Wessex Press, 1909.

Gueber, H. A. *Myths and Legends of the Middle Ages*. London: George Harrap & Co., 1909.

Guest, Lady Charlotte, ed. and trans. *The Mabinogion*. London: Dent; New York: Dutton, 1906.

Halevi, Z'ev ben Shimon. *Kabbalah: Tradition of Hidden Knowledge*. London: Thames & Hudson, 1979.

——. *A Kabbalistic Universe*. Bath, U.K.: Gateway, 1988.

——. *Tree of Life*. Bath, U.K.: Gateway, 1991.

——. *The Way of Kabbalah*. Bath, U.K.: Gateway, 1991.

——. *The Work of the Kabbalist*. Bath, U.K.: Gateway, 1984.

Hall, Manly P. *The Secret Teachings of All Ages*. Los Angeles: Philosophical Research Society, 1977.

Hart, George. *A Dictionary of Egyptian Gods and Goddesses*. London: Routledge and Kegan Paul, 1986.

——. *Egyptian Myths*. London: British Museum, 1990.

Heyneman, Martha. "Dante's Magical Memory Cathedral." *Parabola* XI (1986): 4.

Howard, Michael. *The Wisdom of the Runes*. London: Rider, 1985.

Howard-Gordon, Frances. *Glastonbury Maker of Myths*. Glastonbury, U.K.: Gothic Image, 1982.

Ineni (scribe who lived in the late thirteenth century B.C.E. in Egypt). Papyrus No. 10183 in the British Museum, London.

Jung, Carl G. *Man and His Symbols*. London: Aldus Books and W. H. Allen, 1964.

Lamb, Robert. *World Without Trees*. London: Wildwood House, 1979.

Lang, Andrew. *The Red Fairy Book*. London: Longmans, Green & Co., 1909.

Lang, Jean. *Book of Myths*. Edinburgh: T. C. & E. C. Jack, 1914.

Lang-Sims, Lois. *The Christian Mystery*. London: Allen & Unwin, 1980.

Larousse Encyclopaedia of Mythology. London: Paul Hamlyn, 1960.

Levy, G. R. *The Gate of Horn*. London: Faber, 1948.

Macdowall, M. W. *Asgard of the Gods: The Tales and Traditions of Our Northern Ancestors*. Adapted from the work of Dr. W. Wagner and edited by W. S. W. Anson. London: Swan Sonnenschein, Le Bas & Lowrey, 1886.

Matarasso, P. M., trans. *The Quest for the Holy Grail*. Harmondsworth, U.K.; Baltimore: Penguin, 1969.

Matthews, John. *A Celtic Reader*. London and San Francisco: Harper Collins, Aquarian Press, 1991.

Matthews, W. H. *Mazes and Labyrinths: Their History and Development*. New York: Dover, 1970.

Mercer, S. A. B. *Pyramid Texts*, vol. 4. London: Longmans, 1952.

Moncrieff, A. R. Hope. *Classic Myth and Legend*. London: Gresham, n.d.

Murray, Alexander S. *Manual of Mythology*. New York: Scribner; London: Armstrong & Co., 1876.

Murray, Colin, and Liz Murray. *The Celtic Tree Oracle.* London: Rider, 1988.

Naddair, Kaledon. *Keltic Folk and Faerie Tales: Their Hidden Meaning Explored.* London: Rider, 1987.

Ovid. *Metamorphoses.* Translated by Mary M. Innes. Harmondsworth, U.K., and Baltimore: Penguin, 1968.

Parabola: Myth and the Quest for Meaning. A journal published quarterly by the Society for the Study of Myth and Tradition, New York.

Parrinder, Geoffrey. *African Mythology.* London: Paul Hamlyn, 1967.

Rahner, Hugo. "Christian and Pagan Mysteries," in *Papers from the Eranos Yearbooks, 2: The Mysteries.* Princeton, N.J.: Princeton University Press, 1965.

Reader's Digest Atlas of the Bible. Pleasantville, N.Y.: Readers Digest Association, 1981.

The Rider Encyclopaedia of Mythology. London: Rider, 1989.

Sanders, N. K. *The Epic of Gilgamesh.* Harmondsworth, U.K.: Penguin, 1960, 1964.

Saward, Jeff, and Deb Saward. *Caerdroia.* Thundersley, Benfleet, Essex, U.K. (a journal of research into labyrinths).

Senior, Michael. *Myths of Britain.* London: Book Club Associates, 1979.

Seton-Williams, M. V. *Egyptian Legends and Stories.* London: Rubicon Press, 1910, 1988.

Silcock, Lisa, ed. *The Rainforests: A Celebration.* London: Barrie & Jenkins, 1989.

Simpson, William Kelly, ed. *The Literature of Ancient Egypt.* New Haven, Conn.: Yale University Press, 1972.

Smithett Lewis, Lionel. *Glastonbury: Her Saints, A.D. 37–1539.* London: Research into Lost Knowledge, 1985.

———. *St. Joseph of Arimathea at Glastonbury.* Cambridge: James Clark & Co., 1922, 1955.

Stewart, Bob, and John Matthews. *Legendary Britain.* London: Blandford, 1989.

Temple, Robert, trans. *He Who Saw Everything: A Verse Translation of the Epic of Gilgamesh.* London: Rider, 1991.

Tennyson, Alfred, Lord. *Poetical Works of Alfred, Lord Tennyson.* London and New York: Eyre & Spottiswoode, n.d.

Thomas, E. W. *Bushman Stories.* Oxford: Oxford University Press, 1950.

Toulson, Shirley. *The Winter Solstice.* London: Jill Norman & Hobhouse, 1981.

Virgil. *The Aeneid.* Translated by W. F. Jackson Knight. Harmondsworth, U.K.: Penguin, 1972.

Walker, Barbara G. *The Woman's Encyclopaedia of Myths and Secrets.* San Francisco: Harper & Row, 1983.

Wilberforce, William. *Diary.* 1787.

Wolkstein, Diane, and S. N. Kramer. *Inanna: Queen of Heaven and Earth.* San Francisco: Harper & Row, 1983; London: Century Hutchinson, 1984.

Wordsworth, William. *The Poetical Works of William Wordsworth.* London and New York: Ward, Locke & Co., Ltd., n.d.

Index